The Landlord's Handbook

An essential guide to successful residential letting

by Leon Hopkins

HARRIMAN HOUSE LTD

3A Penns Road
Petersfield
Hampshire
GU32 2EW
GREAT BRITAIN

Tel: +44 (0)1730 233870
Fax: +44 (0)1730 233880
Email: enquiries@harriman-house.com
Website: www.harriman-house.com

First published in Great Britain in 2010
Copyright © Harriman House 2010

The right of Leon Hopkins to be identified as Author has been asserted in accordance with the Copyright, Design and Patents Act 1988.

ISBN: 978-0857190-18-5

Printed and bound in Great Britain by CPI Antony Rowe, Chippenham.

Contents

Making the Life of a Landlord Easier

Being a landlord is both rewarding and demanding.

Good landlords know that providing housing for tenants can bring handsome financial returns, as well as the satisfaction of fulfilling a social need.

They also know that it is not always easy being a landlord. Not all tenants are as well behaved as they might be; a few may be downright devious. And then there are the 50-plus Acts of Parliament and 70-plus sets of regulations concerning private rentals that landlords have to know about and comply with.

Aided by the advent of *buy-to-let* mortgages, many people who would not previously have considered renting property have moved into the market because of its investment potential. There are also significant numbers of *accidental landlords* who have either inherited property they cannot live in but prefer to keep, or have a property that they could not sell when moving.

This book is designed to help them all, debutant landlords and seasoned investors alike, by providing a concise summary of the ins and outs of being a landlord, the decisions to be made and actions to be taken – and how best to approach and deal with them all. It tackles business and financial risks, as well as legal requirements and regulatory demands.

A guide to the essentials

Starting with the question 'why let residential property?', the guide moves on to look at such topics as finance, suitable property, licensing, finding suitable tenants, tenancy agreements, possession procedures, repairs, grants, taxation and insurance – in short, all the major areas of importance to landlords in their letting businesses.

With so many pieces of legislation to deal with, any guide could easily become too detailed. My aim has been to give an overview rather than a legal treatise, and to provide easy access to a host of references for those who need to look up more detailed aspects of legislation and official guidance.

Primarily I have dealt with the law as it currently exists in England and Wales, whilst endeavouring throughout to point landlords from Scotland and Northern Ireland to major differences in the law that affect them, and also to sources of more detailed information. Although the guide covers the main areas of legal responsibility, it is certainly not intended to be an exhaustive explanation of all requirements faced by private landlords. And it is not a substitute for legal advice – landlords faced with unusual or complicated circumstances, or who are unsure about any aspects of what might be required, should always seek professional advice.

Throughout I have included examples of actual situations that illustrate the demands, and sometimes the pitfalls, of being a landlord.

My intention has been to provide a primer for newcomer landlords, and a reliable reference book for old hands – an accessible, dependable guide to the essentials of letting, in order to make life as a landlord that bit easier.

For this reason I have also included a 'Jargon Buster' section, starting on page 237, giving brief explanations of the more common of the many technical terms that landlords may come across in their letting businesses.

Tenants and prospective tenants will also find essential information in the guide about what is expected of landlords, about required property and safety standards, and their own legal rights and responsibilities when taking on tenancies.

LH, June 2010

Leon Hopkins is editor of the website:
www.residentiallandlord.co.uk

His previous titles include *The Hundredth Year, Budgeting for Business, Cash Flow and How to Improve It* and *The Audit Report.*

1.

Why (and How to) Let Residential Property?

For most people, letting is primarily a financial proposition; a means of making money and accumulating wealth. And if done properly, it can certainly live up to financial expectations. Among those attracted to the rental market are some high-profile sportsmen and women, including, famously, former Liverpool striker Robbie Fowler, who is reputed to own over 100 residential lets in the Oldham area.

Landlords – whether they own one flat or a portfolio to rival Fowler's – benefit from both rental income and the rising value of the properties they own. Although in 2010 house prices dipped 10% below the peak reached in October 2007, figures produced by the mortgage lender Nationwide suggested that even this meant that, over the previous 15 years as a whole, house prices had more than trebled.

Landlords who owned residential property during that period have done very well. Despite economic difficulties in the 2007-2009 recession and subsequently, relatively few landlords sold up; most retained or even increased their property portfolios – in the expectation of rising property prices in the future.

Those who had not overstretched themselves by simply borrowing too much were well able to sit out the downturn; partly because when the housing market is flat or falling fewer people are interested in buying their own homes, more decide to rent, and higher demand translates into rising rents.

There is also a social aspect to letting – providing much needed housing. Although a few landlords try to cut corners and earn themselves a bad name as a result, very many more

> **Landlords – whether they own one flat or a portfolio – benefit from both rental income and the rising value of the properties they own.**

take pride in the socially responsible role they have to play. It is not only people who cannot afford to buy who decide to rent property. In fact a very large proportion of the population choose to rent at some point of their lives – for personal or family reasons, for work or for study.

Renting also leaves people relatively free to move around from town to town: meaning that the rental sector contributes to the economic health of the country by helping to sustain a more mobile workforce.

The rise of regulation

However, because housing is so central to the wellbeing of families, letting is an area that is highly regulated – and has become more so over recent years.

Rented houses must be of an adequate standard and must certainly not expose tenants, or anybody else for that matter, to any dangers to life, limb or health. Neither will the community as a whole, or the courts in particular, tolerate tenants being thrown out of their rented homes without good reason, and even then not without first going through formal procedures. Nor should tenants be harassed or otherwise prevented from the "quiet enjoyment" of their rented homes (to use the phrase enshrined in decades of English Common Law).

The law does *assure* landlords who let property on the basis of assured tenancies that their properties will be returned to them when tenancy agreements end or have been breached. But should it become necessary to terminate a tenancy, this must be done strictly within the procedures laid down.

Landlords who transgress these rules can find themselves in considerable trouble; not just facing fines but also in some instances criminal proceedings that can result in a jail sentence.

Common and business sense

The implications for landlords are that they must treat letting in a businesslike way. They need to ensure that they are compliant with the many requirements of the law; and they must maintain adequate records, sufficiently detailed for their tax returns, and to be able to justify their actions should these be called into question in any way – as well as, if necessary, to counter any unjustified claims made by tenants or their representatives.

Neither should new landlords think that letting is a get-rich-quick route to prosperity. Robbie Fowler's buy-to-let investments have caused his name to appear high on various *rich lists*, but he did not achieve this overnight.

Sensible landlords do not go for the quick kill. They choose their properties carefully for their letting potential and maintain them well, knowing that they will own them for some time. They also choose their tenants with care and value good relations with good tenants.

Whether to Incorporate or Not

Some buy-to-let investments, including some high profile ventures, have gone horribly wrong. Among these is Imagine Homes Limited, the buy-to-let business once run by Grant Bovey, the husband of television presenter Anthea Turner. He had been backed by HBOS, the bank now owned by Lloyds Banking Group, and had grown the company at a ferocious pace after setting it up in 2003. At one point Imagine Homes was reputed to be the largest buy-to-let business in the country, managing over 1000 lets. But the company was caught out by the banking crisis in 2007-2009 and the slump in the housing market that followed. By May 2009 it had been placed into administration.

In his report of July 2009 the administrator reported that the company owned residential properties with a book value of just under £77m, but it was estimated these could be sold for only £11m. Overall the company had a shortfall running to over £100m. Although the business was run via a limited company, Bovey lost out personally as well.

The spread of risk, tax and profits

One of the first decisions new landlords must make is whether to run their letting businesses as personal undertakings, partnerships or by means of limited companies.

Most buy-to-let-landlords trade as individuals or partners – often in business partnership with their wives or husbands – which allows them to share both an interest in their properties and their tax allowances.

Individuals and partners

Trading as an individual means the person concerned receives – and is taxed on – all the profits. It also means that he or she bears all the financial risk. So if the business should fail for some reason, or, say, a substantial legal claim should arise, the financial responsibility will fall entirely on that person.

Having a partner or partners means the profits and risks are shared between the partners (although partners are *jointly and severally* liable for claims against the business, a legal concept that means if one or more of the partners is unable to pay his or her share, the other partner or partners have to make up the difference).

There can be tax advantages to married couples or civil partners in becoming business partners if one would not otherwise use up his or her personal allowances, lower rate tax bands, or capital gains tax exemptions. By having a share of the profits this spare allowance, lower rate or exemption is not left to go to waste. Taken together the tax paid would then be less than if all gains went to one partner only.

Limited companies

Trading as a limited company means that, in theory at least, the risks are limited to the share capital of the company – generally the money committed at the outset. So there is no personal liability for business debts beyond the initial capital invested. However, this protection can be easily overridden by a requirement from lenders for personal guarantees. And should things go wrong, the owners and directors will have to settle any personal indebtedness to the company that has arisen.

If a limited company owns the letting business and the properties it controls, it is a relatively simple matter to change the ownership of part or all of the business without disrupting its operations or having to sell off some or all of the properties. Bringing in new investors, giving away or selling part of the business, or dealing with inheritances can all be dealt with by a transfer of shares (rather than of properties).

Corporation tax

Different tax rules apply to companies than to individual traders or partners in a business.

Income and capital gains are taxed according to corporation tax rules. As rates and details change from time to time, this can be an advantage or disadvantage but the general principle is that the company pays corporation tax on profits and gains at the rates applying at the time. The after-tax figure remains the property of the company. Money can only be taken out by the owners as wages (if they become employees) – in which case the wages are an allowable charge against profits but must bear income tax and

National Insurance – or as dividends. Dividends are paid net of a tax deduction but there is no National Insurance to pay.

Companies can be purchased ready-made (i.e. created by company formation specialists) relatively cheaply, or landlords can form their own companies (the Companies House website, **www.companieshouse.gov.uk**, explains how). Either way, once a company is in place there has to be at least one director and company secretary responsible for administration of company documentation including annual returns (for which there is a small annual filing fee) and company accounts. Once filed at Companies House, these documents are available for inspection by anybody willing to pay the nominal inspection fee.

* * *

Whether or not it would be best to trade as a sole trader, partnership or limited company will depend upon both current personal circumstances and future aspirations. Landlords who are uncertain about whether or not incorporation would be advantageous to themselves should seek advice from an accountant or lawyer.

One point to bear in mind is that although the legal status of a letting business can be changed at a later date (it is generally easier to turn a personally owned business or a partnership into a limited company rather than the other way around), this will crystallise values and will almost certainly result in a tax liability. So it is important to think about long-term aims and aspirations and to set up the letting business in a way that best matches these in a way and which is most likely to help make the business successful.

2.

Buy-to-Let Finance

Most house buyers rely on mortgage finance to make their purchases and landlords are no exception. However, consumer mortgages are generally not suitable for the purchase of rental property. At the very least, those who become landlords by default (because they are obliged to move for one reason or another but cannot sell their existing property) must seek their mortgage lender's permission to let the premises. More than likely they, like landlords buying property specifically to rent, will be required to switch to a *buy-to-let* mortgage.

These mortgages have only existed for a decade or so – previously landlords would have required a commercial mortgage – but the market has grown quickly. The Council of Mortgage Lenders, which has only collected statistics related to buy-to-let mortgages since 2006, says that at the end of 2008 there were 1.56m buy-to-let mortgages in place, with a total of £138bn outstanding – around 10% of total mortgage lending in the UK.

From the beginning of 2009 buy-to-let mortgage lending remained *broadly flat*, with 22,000 loans worth £2.1bn being made in the first three months of 2010. But although the number of potential lenders contracted as a result of the credit crunch and all that ensued, there were still estimated to be over 400 lenders in the market.

While buy-to-let mortgages once suffered lower arrears than retail mortgages, in 2008 the position was reversed. At the end of 2008 there were 219,000 buy-to-let mortgages in arrears by three months or more. Since then low interest rates had contributed to *a modest improvement* in buy-to-let arrears. At the end of March 2010 the number of loans with arrears of more than 1.5% of the mortgage balance totalled 19,300 (just over 1.5% of all buy-to-let loans – down from a high of just under 2.5% a year earlier). CML said the reasons for the increase in arrears included over valuation of properties at the outset so as to obtain loans in excess of the value of the property (in fact fraud), payment problems on the part of landlords and void periods when rental properties remained empty with no rental income. So the lesson is that prudent landlords should not overstretch themselves by borrowing to the hilt and should always work on the assumption that they may well face void periods from time to time.

A halfway house

Buy-to-let mortgages are something of a halfway house between consumer and commercial mortgages. They tend to have longer repayment periods than commercial mortgages and are for larger percentages of the purchase price (higher *loan to value*, or LTV), but are more expensive that consumer mortgages.

- Typically buy-to-let mortgages are limited to 75% or 85% of LTV. Higher figures have been achieved in the past. Lenders take into account expected rental income and will expect this to exceed repayments, typically by 25% or even 50%.

- Lenders may restrict the amount they will lend per property – although this might be as high as £1m – or per portfolio.

Landlords who have borrowed heavily against their properties – negotiating high LTVs, or becoming *highly geared* in financial parlance – tend to do well (at least on paper) while property prices move upwards. This is because whilst they may have paid for only, say, 25% of the property, they benefit from 100% of any rise in value.

The downside with this strategy is, of course, that they remain committed to high regular payments whether or not their properties have tenants. And if things go wrong, say because the property cannot be let, or tenants abscond, it can take some time to sell the property to raise cash – even in a rising market, and especially in a falling market. So the higher the gearing, the higher the potential risk.

Which Mortgage is the Best for You?

Buy-to-let mortgages come in a number of different forms: fixed-rate mortgages, variable-rate mortgages, capped, low-start, interest-only or interest-plus-capital-repayment.

The terms over which fixed or other rates apply can vary from as little as one year to the whole term of the mortgage. There may well be penalties for paying off the mortgage before the agreed term has expired, or for switching to an alternative mortgage. Which mortgage will be the most suitable for you will depend on many factors. This will include what is on offer, and to whom, at the time the money is needed (buy-to-let mortgage lenders tend to change their packages fairly frequently and many will target particular parts of the market). It will also involve your assessment of the way interest rates are likely to move, or whether you prefer to take interest rate movements out of the equation to some extent, by opting for a fixed rate that will not change for a specified period, no matter how Bank of England or interbank lending rates change.

- Landlords who expect interest rates to go up and who like to know that their outgoings are fixed are more likely to choose fixed-rate products. Those who judge that interest rates are moving down are more likely to favour variable-rate or tracker products.

Landlords in search of buy-to-let mortgage finance will naturally want the best deals available. What those might be will depend upon their own circumstances, their business credentials as landlords, the amount they wish to borrow, over what period, and the LTV this represents. The best deals, of course, will go to those landlords who lenders perceive to be less of a risk – experienced landlords with established property portfolios, whose borrowing represents relatively low LTV with good rental cover.

Landlords can approach lenders directly or use one of the specialist buy-to-let mortgage brokers out there. Either way it is likely that an arrangement fee, probably between 1% and 3%, will be charged (usually this is added to the loan).

As a starting point for finding a suitable buy-to-let mortgage, the website Residential Landlord maintains a list of current mortgage offers.

www.residentiallandlord.co.uk/buytoletmortgagelenders.htm

Potential problems

Landlords do sometimes overstretch themselves and can end up having their properties repossessed. In the first three months of 2010 there were no less that 1,400 buy-to-let property foreclosures. And there were another 11,200 cases in which a receiver of rent had been appointed – a not dissimilar process to foreclosure, in which the mortgage lender appoints a receiver to collect the rent and pass it directly to the mortgage lender.

Landlords can run into difficulties with mortgage repayments when they cannot find suitable tenants, or sometimes when tenants living in their properties suddenly stop paying the rent for one reason or another. This can be because of illness, unemployment or some personal problem. Some tenants are simply delinquent. And it can take even the most alert landlord some time to evict tenants who are unable or unwilling to pay the rent and to re-let the property.

Landlords need to have reasonable contingency plans to cover such circumstances. As Chapter 3 suggests, some of this ideally needs to be addressed when selecting suitable property in the first place.

When Bailiffs Come Knocking

It is important that landlords who finance their property purchases by means of mortgages either obtain buy-to-let mortgages or (if, for example, they are letting a property in which they originally lived) obtain permission to rent from their mortgage company. If they do not, they are placing themselves in an awkward position with their mortgage company, which will hardly do their future credit standing much good, and will also be letting down their tenants.

It is claimed that over 300,000 households are rented from landlords who should have, but have not, obtained their mortgage lender's permission to let the property.

The tenants of these landlords are in a precarious position because, in theory at least, should the mortgage company repossess the property, they can be evicted without notice.

The law is in fact being changed. The Mortgage Repossessions (Protection of Tenants etc) Act 2010, passed just prior to the 2010 General Election, gives *unauthorised* tenants the right to be heard at any possession hearings brought by mortgage lenders, and the Court the right to postpone execution of possession for up to two months. If a lender obtains a possession order, it can only be enforced if proper notice is given.

In fact, at time of writing, the Act had yet to come into force since a commencement order was required.

Tenants of landlords who have obtained permission to let from their mortgage lender, or who have financed the purchase of the property via a buy-to-let mortgage, put themselves and their tenants in a different position – since usually the tenancy will be binding on the lender, who has to honour the contract. This usually means the tenant will have at least two months' notice.

Landlords intent on running their lettings businesses on a proper footing will certainly make sure their mortgage lenders know they are letting their properties and would be best advised to include a paragraph in their tenancy agreements informing tenants that the property is subject to a mortgage granted before the beginning of the agreement and that in certain circumstances the mortgage lender could become entitled to sell the property.

The clause should give notice that in such circumstances *Ground 2* for possession (one of the statutory grounds for possession that the Courts must accept) will be used. Prior notice is required to use this route to possession and as the agreement contains that notice the tenants could be given two months notice to quit.

3.

Suitable Properties

If being a private landlord is a business, then the rental homes the business has to offer are its products. Rentals have to be *sold* to tenants not just once; potentially each property has to be marketed every six months (the minimum length of an assured shorthold tenancy agreement and the default period usually written into such agreements; although tenants often stay longer by running on their agreement – when they have what is known as a *periodic tenancy* – or signing a new tenancy agreement). So it is important for landlords to buy properties that have strong selling points.

Who Are You Renting To?

Different types of tenant have different priorities. So identifying a suitable rental property to purchase begins with deciding to whom you wish to rent (the market).

Tied up with this, and essential to the whole proposition, are the financial implications – can the property be let to the sort of tenants you have in mind at an economically viable rent?

In the past, and almost certainly in the future, landlords have benefited from rising house prices, so that some of their returns can be expected in the form of capital gains. But capital gains are only converted into cash at the time a property is sold. This means landlords have to strike a balance between expected rental income and expected cash outgoings – including mortgage repayments. And if they are prudent they will leave themselves a comfortable margin to allow for void periods, emergencies when their properties cannot be used for some reason, or when tenants refuse to pay or to leave.

The choice of preferred market is wide, ranging from students to professionals, from singles to married couples with families, from personal to corporate rentals. Each group will have their own requirements regarding rent levels, type of accommodation (flat, town house, house with garden, with or without garaging), standard of accommodation, fixtures and fittings and contents (if included), location, local transport and proximity to shops, cinemas, schools and the like.

In university towns and elsewhere, *houses in multiple occupation* (HMOs) have been a popular choice for some landlords since they generate income from a number of tenants living in individual rooms. However, landlords should be aware that special rules apply to such properties, with local authorities taking a proactive interest in the standards of accommodation and in some instances landlord licences are required. This is covered in more depth later.

Researching your market

Prudent landlords begin their property search with some research into the market in the location in which they intend to buy. Local press and local letting agents can provide a starting point for assessing the rental property most in demand, the level of rents that are currently being achieved and the likely purchase price of such properties. It would also be helpful to know such local details as:

- major employers and their location

- bus and train routes

- whether or not there is a university in the town or nearby

- where the most popular schools are located

- where the parks, libraries and leisure facilities are

- what the local level of unemployment is

And as much more of the like as can easily be discovered.

It is important to match the size of property to the target market. In general the average size of households is declining as it becomes more common for people to live on their own or as single parents. Singletons or young couples without children will not want to pay for larger properties with rooms they are unlikely to use.

Another decision is whether to let your property furnished or unfurnished. At one time this would have affected the legal standing of the let, but not any more. Your primary decision is whether a furnished property is more or less likely to attract the type of tenants you are targeting. The standard of furnishing will obviously also be important in this respect. There is no legal definition of what constitutes *furnished*, *unfurnished* or *part-furnished* accommodation. Whether what you do attracts those target tenants will be down to your taste and judgement and to how well you describe exactly what it is you are offering in your marketing.

As a rule of thumb, it is generally thought that unfurnished lets attract tenants more likely to stay for some time – after all, moving will cost them something. They may also be more inclined to take care with the contents of their home. On the other hand, as a move will be a major event for replacement tenants, it may take longer to arrange new lets – meaning increased void periods.

There are one or two other considerations to be borne in mind. If you do decide on furnished accommodation you might (depending on the local market) be able charge a slightly higher rent. But you must make sure that everything you supply meets current safety standards (of which, more later), and you will have to insure the contents. You will be able to charge wear and tear of the furnishings against your income when accounting for tax.

But remember – whatever furniture and equipment is there at the outset of a let and listed on the inventory must be present and in good working order (replaced if needs be) for the use of your tenants throughout the whole of the tenancy. If something stops functioning or becomes unusable as a consequence of normal *wear and tear*, it will be up to the landlord to put things right. So, for example, if a hot water boiler breaks down, this will usually be something the landlord will have to pay for to put right. But if there are breakages, these will be for the tenant to rectify by replacement of the broken item, or items – or if the worst comes to the worst, by deduction of an appropriate amount from the tenancy deposit.

Gardens are a particular issue. Most people like gardens; fewer like the upkeep they require. Landlords who buy properties with large gardens need to be sure this is a renting plus-point, and, if so, should decide how the garden will be maintained.

Flats in particular

Such considerations have led some landlords to prefer flats to houses – all the exterior maintenance, including that of any communal garden space, is usually taken care of by subcontractors as part of the leasehold or commonhold agreement. But flats have their own problems as investments. The tenure, the legal status of ownership, can vary. The flat may be leasehold (in effect rental of the property from the outright owner, or freeholder, usually at a fairly nominal rent – the ground rent – for a considerable number of years, often 99 years or 999 years). Or it could be commonhold (each flat owner having a share in the company that owns the freehold), for example.

There will certainly be conditions and arrangements for service charges written into the purchase agreement to cover such matters as maintenance of common parts of the block in which the flat is situated, including arrangements for keeping stairs, hallways, lifts, gardens (if any), the exterior of the building and associated car parks and garages in appropriate condition.

The lease or commonhold agreement will have to be checked carefully to make sure letting is permitted (it may only be permitted with the freeholder's or head leaseholder's permission, for example).

Also, the level of service charge needs to be checked as some flats attract high service charges, which of course must also be recouped via rent. This means landlords must be sure that the rent will still be competitive enough to attract the type of tenants they are seeking. They also need to prepare for having to pay the service charge during void periods when they have no rental income because one tenant has left and a replacement has yet to be found.

With modern flats being built in many towns, a reasonable number of landlords have bought units *off plan* in recent years – in other words they have agreed to buy even before the properties were built. Buying this way often comes with a discount. But the problem has been that, with a substantial number of flats coming onto the market all at the same time, they have sometimes proved difficult to let.

In some instances developers have offered *guaranteed rents* to landlord investors for a period after completion. But given that developers are then committed to finding tenants or making up the difference themselves, they may well offer the flats at rock bottom rents – meaning this seemingly favourable arrangement can have the effect of keeping initial rent levels low.

Natural hazards

Vulnerability of properties to natural hazards, particularly to flooding, is another factor that should be considered. When a property is let, a contract is created between tenants and landlord for the supply of housing. If a property becomes uninhabitable because of flooding, landlords are still obliged to provide housing for the period of the contract. Adequate insurance to cover the additional costs involved in supplying alternative accommodation, not to mention repairs, is obviously needed.

Even so, it would probably have been better had the property not been bought in the first place – not least because its long-term value is likely to be affected and the cost of its insurance pushed up.

Flood risks for areas can be checked on the Environment Agency's website (**www.environment-agency.gov.uk**).

Housing standards

Rental properties must reach certain standards so when looking at potential buys it is important to know if they already meet requirements or, if not, the likely cost of repairs and upgrades.

At one time, rigid housing fitness standards were laid down. In 2006, however, these were replaced by the more fluid Housing Health and Safety Rating System (HHSRS). This is the system that councils use when inspecting property because of a complaint or for some other reason, such as granting a licence (see page 25).

Landlords generally are not required to have their properties inspected before letting although there are special rules that apply to houses in multiple-occupation, and to licensing and accreditation schemes. For example, local authorities must satisfy themselves that there are no *category one* hazards within properties before issuing an HMO licence. Category one hazards are those risks that could lead to death, permanent paralysis below the neck, regular severe pneumonia, or 80% burns or worse. Landlords should be aware that if for some reason their properties are inspected and deemed not to comply with any of the HHSRS in some material way, they will have to make improvements. According to the government booklet on the subject[1], the HHSRS

---

[1] Housing Health and Safety Rating System: Enforcement Guidance (**www.communities.gov.uk/publications/housing/housinghealth2**) and Housing Health and Safety Rating System – Guidance for Landlords and Property Related Professional (**www.communities.gov.uk/publications/housing/housinghealth**).

system is based on the principle that any residential premises should provide a safe and healthy environment for any potential occupier or visitor. As well as providing protection from the environment, dwellings should be capable of being occupied safely and healthily by a range of households from a spectrum of lifestyles and age profiles.

HHSRS

Rental property must be safe to occupy and whether or not it is safe is not left for landlords to decide. Rather, their properties must be in compliance with the Housing Health and Safety Rating System (HHSRS). This is a risk-based method of assessment which councils are required to use when evaluating a property's safety. This may be undertaken following a complaint, or for other reasons, such as when a HMO licence is applied for.

HHSRS is primarily concerned with those matters which can properly be considered the responsibility of the owner (or landlord). Generally these include the provision, state and proper working order of:

1. (a) Exterior and structural elements of the dwelling; and

    (b) installations within and associated with the dwelling for:

    - the supply and use of water, gas and electricity

    - personal hygiene, sanitation and drainage

    - food safety

    - ventilation

    - space heating

    - heating water.

There are 29 headings under which risk is assessed:

1. Damp and mould growth
2. Excess cold
3. Excess heat
4. Asbestos (and MMF)
5. Biocides
6. Carbon monoxide and fuel combustion products
7. Lead
8. Radiation
9. Uncombusted fuel gas
10. Volatile organic compounds
11. Crowding and space
12. Entry by intruders
13. Lighting
14. Noise protection
15. Domestic hygiene, pests and refuse
16. Food safety
17. Personal hygiene, sanitation and drainage
18. Water supply for domestic purpose
19. Falls associated with baths
20. Falling on level surfaces
21. Falling on stairs, etc
22. Falling between levels
23. Electrical hazards
24. Fire
25. Flames, hot surfaces
26. Collision and entrapment
27. Explosions
28. Position and operability of amenities
29. Structural collapse and failing elements

Should hazards under any of these headings be detected in a council inspection, the council must go on to assess the likelihood of those hazards crystallising and causing harm – and the probable severity of any such harm. The assessment culminates in a *hazard rating* for the property.

There are four classes of harm, of which *category one* is the most severe. These are risks that could lead to death, permanent paralysis below the neck, regular severe pneumonia, or 80% burns or worse. Local authorities have a duty to take action on category-one hazards and the power to take action on category-two hazards. This applies to all properties, whether owner-occupied or rented, although landlords are the most likely to be affected.

In most cases a local authority, having found a material hazard in a rented property, will first contact the landlord or agent and request work be undertaken to remove or reduce the hazard. If no action is taken, the request may be followed by a legal notice either requiring works to be done or restricting use of the property. Should a legal notice not be complied with, the local authority will have the power to prosecute the owners of the property and carry out the works itself and recover all costs.

Where a hazard has been identified as providing an imminent risk of harm or requiring urgent attention, a legal notice may be served without prior notification.

General duty of care

Quite apart from these standards, landlords have a general duty of care towards tenants. Cavalier attitudes towards hazards could easily lead, in cases of accidents, to claims from tenants. So care should be taken to ensure that properties intended for rental are equipped as far as reasonably possible with safety devices such as smoke detectors on every floor (a legal requirement for all residential properties built after 1992) and that there are no inherently hazardous items (such as glazed doors that have not been fitted with safety glass, or lead plumbing).

It is important to know that more stringent requirements apply to properties intended to be let as *houses in multiple occupation* (student lets are typically HMOs, for example) and to their landlords – see the next section for more on this. It is, for example, often a requirement that fire doors are fitted in such properties.

Long-term potential

Besides letting potential, landlords should also have an eye for the long-term potential of the property. These are examples of the kinds of questions you should be asking yourself:

- Is its value likely to increase because it is of a type that is likely to increase in demand (perennially fashionable, or similar to other local successes)?

- Could selling be a problem because, perhaps, the property is in a part of town that is in decline?

- Could value be affected because it is in an area dependent on one large employer whose industry is in decline or vulnerable to the pressures of overseas competitors (so that at some point it may be forced to close, to outsource production, or to re-locate)?

- Is the property in an area that is vulnerable to flooding?

- Are there, or might there be, local development plans for new facilities?

- Are there, or might there be, new roads in the area, or even tram routes?

As pointed out earlier, capital appreciation accounts for an important, sometimes the most important, element of financial gain from letting. So choosing and buying wisely, and choosing the right time to sell, are important skills to develop.

Auction

Some landlords elect to buy their properties at auction. For those with the wherewithal to do so – chiefly a cool head and the financial means in place in advance – there is no doubt that there are bargain properties to be had. What's more, the buying process is relatively quick.

There are drawbacks, of course. First of all, as said, anybody bidding for property at auction has to be in a position to move ahead immediately – the money has to be as good as in the bank. Usually you will be asked to pay a 10% deposit on the auction day and the balance within 28 days. There is also, of course, the possibility of getting carried away in a bidding competition and not getting such a bargain after all.

But even more to the point, properties go to auction for a reason. This could be that they cannot be sold quickly in the normal way. It might be that the previous owners had their property repossessed and the finance company is not willing to wait the few months, sometimes the numerous months, it takes to sell through an estate agent. *Or* it could be that the property is in a poor state and needs work to bring it up to standard. So go in with your eyes open.

There are plenty of property auctions up and down the country – you can search Google for 'property auctions', although you can shortcut this by looking at the list published on **www.residentiallandlord.co.uk**. This means you can turn up prepared, having scanned the catalogue of the chosen auction, viewed any possible buys and estimated what will have to be spent to make the property suitable to let (when you view the property it might be a good idea to take a trusted builder along for an expert view on likely costs). You should also register with the auction house and obtain legal packs for the properties you think you would like to buy. It is also a good idea to set the upper price you are prepared to meet for each possible property, and to stick to it.

Some auctioneers advise attending one or two auctions just to see how the process works before going in earnest. It would be wise to seek legal advice before bidding for a property and to conduct legal property searches. If you do things correctly you could end up with a bargain.

The Royal Institution of Chartered Surveyors, at **www.rics.org**, has further advice.

Know your market – the rise in renter diversity

When Jim Holden got a new job he decided he and his partner could afford a better house than the one they had been renting for the past year. This was a terraced property, over 100 years old. One of the two upstairs bedrooms had been converted into a bathroom, and the kitchen was a little pokey. And, with early starts on the cards, he wanted to be closer to his new employer on the other side of the city, or at least nearer to a convenient bus route.

After a short search, Jim's girlfriend Jenny found them a loft conversion in a new docklands development. She liked the lively atmosphere, the large number of local shops and restaurants, and the roomier accommodation. All in all, they decided it was worth paying the higher rent and moved in.

Jim and Jenny, both in their mid-twenties, are among the three million private renters in the UK, and are typical of many. They were just the sort of tenants the landlord had been targeting.

The three million estimate comes from a 2009 government report on housing in England, conducted over 2007-08, which suggests that almost one-in-seven households rent their homes from private landlords.

Reflecting the buy-to-let boom, the figure was substantially more than the 2.1 million living in privately rented accommodation ten years earlier.

Renting was found to be more common in London than any other region, with one-in-five households living in privately rented accommodation. On average tenants were getting younger – four-in-ten private renters were aged between 25 and 29, double the proportion in that age range five years earlier.

Six-in-ten households that had started renting only in the last year (2008) were aged between 16 and 24. People who moved into rented accommodation after having been owner-occupiers were, unsurprisingly, more likely to be older, with nine-in-ten aged between 25 and 54 – possibly reflecting the breakdown of relationships, the report surmised.

Rents across the country averaged £136 per week for assured shorthold tenancies (the default form of tenancy – of which there is much more later), £85 per week for regulated and resident landlord tenancies. There were considerable regional variations. Average rents in the South were £158 per week, in the North £93 per week. In London the average was £208 per week.

One-in-five private renters were receiving housing benefit – down from nearer one-in-three ten years earlier. Lone parent tenants were the group most likely to be receiving housing benefit; seven-in-ten relied on this support.

Four-in-ten private renters had been in their current home for less than a year. Most had moved on from a previous let. The most cited reasons for moving, in descending order, were to find different sized accommodation, to be nearer a workplace, and to move to a better area. Most moved less than five miles from their previous let.

4.

Houses in Multiple Occupation (HMOs)

There are special rules applying to houses in multiple occupation (HMOs) – houses let to groups of unrelated people who, typically, have a bedroom each but share all the other rooms.

Student lets are the classic example of an HMO. But despite *The Young Ones'* image of mayhem and squalor, they have been popular with landlords because the rent coming from, say, six bedrooms let separately tends to be more than could be achieved from letting the house as a whole. But, perhaps because houses in multiple occupation tend to be larger, older, houses – often of three storeys or more – a few have proved themselves to be fire traps.

Clearly it is not acceptable that anybody's life be put in danger by inadequate fire protection – something that is underlined if tenants are young students with their whole future ahead of them. This is why in 2000 the Scottish Executive introduced a licensing requirement for anybody intending to let a house in Scotland as an HMO (failure to obtain such a licence is a criminal offence).In Scotland the definition of an HMO is a house (which includes any part of a building occupied as a separate dwelling) which is the only or principal residence of three or more qualifying persons from three or more families ('families' include unmarried and same-sex couples but not cousins).

There are a few exceptions, such as for care homes. Details of the requirement can be found at **www.scotland.gov.uk** – search for 'Houses in Multiple Occupation: A Guide for Landlords').

In 2004 the British government followed the Scottish example and introduced a licensing requirement for larger houses in multiple occupation in England and Wales, along with complicated (but different) definitions of what constitutes a house in multiple occupation and which properties, within this definition, now require licences.

Northern Ireland had a voluntary licensing scheme from 2004, and has a Statutory Registration Scheme for HMOs capable of occupation by more than 10 people and benefiting from an HMO. It applies to specified areas only. (Go to **www.nihe.gov.uk** and search for 'The Statutory Registration Scheme for Houses in Multiple Occupation in Northern Ireland', and 'Good Management Practice Guide for Houses in Multiple Occupation'.)

The remainder of this section deals with the requirements now in force in England and Wales.

* * *

Definition

The Housing Act 2004 (which came into effect in 2006 and 2007) says that a house or flat is deemed to be a house in multiple occupation if it is let to three or more tenants who form two or more households, and the tenants share a kitchen, bathroom or toilet. This includes houses that have been converted into bedsits or flats with shared facilities and which are let to three or more tenants who form two or more households. It also covers houses converted into entirely self-contained flats but whose conversion did not meet the 1991 Building Regulations and when completed more than a third have been let out on short-term tenancies (building regulations are national rules, separate from planning consent, that have to be complied with in construction or conversions). Another stipulation is that the property is used solely or mainly to house tenants who use it as their only or main home. This includes accommodation let to students in higher or further education, to asylum seekers and migrant and seasonal workers, and accommodation used as a refuge for people escaping domestic violence are all considered to meet this criterion, alongside more conventional full-time renters.

Excluded are buildings managed or controlled by local authorities, registered social landlords, the police or fire services, a health service body, student accommodation managed and controlled by educational establishments, buildings occupied principally for the purposes of a religious community whose principal occupation is "prayer, contemplation, education or the relief of suffering", and buildings occupied by their owners.

For the purposes of the definition, a *household* is generally a single person or couple (including same-sex couples) and their children or others, such as carers, who are employed by them.

For the full definition of what in law constitutes an HMO consult the Housing Act 2004 and accompanying notes, available from **www.opsi.gov.uk**.

Licences and living standards

HMO properties must meet prescribed standards laid down in the statutory instrument, 'The Licensing and Management of Houses in Multiple Occupation and Other Houses (Miscellaneous Provisions) (England) Regulations 2006' (also available from **www.opsi.gov.uk**).

Those that are of three storeys or more, occupied by two or more households comprising a total of five or more people, are required to have a licence issued by the relevant local authority. If they do not do so their landlords could find themselves fined up to £20,000 and unable to collect their rents.

" HMOs that are of three storeys or more, occupied by two or more households comprising a total of five or more people, are required to have a licence issued by the relevant local authority. **"**

In addition to mandatory licensing of larger HMOs, the law also allows for *additional licensing* where local authorities consider that a significant proportion of HMOs in their area are giving rise to problems for the occupants or the public because they are not being managed sufficiently well. A number of local authorities have applied for and obtained such additional licensing powers, so it is important for landlords investing in HMOs to check the current position locally.

Whether or not a licence is required, there are a number of basic living standards that must be met:

- All units of living accommodation in HMOs must be equipped with adequate means of space heating.

- Where there are four or fewer occupiers of the HMO and all or some of the units do not contain bath and toilet facilities, there must be at least one bathroom with a fixed bath or shower and a toilet for general use (which may be situated in the bathroom). Where there are five or more occupiers sharing those facilities, there must be one separate toilet with wash hand basin for every five sharing occupiers and at least one bathroom (which may contain a toilet) with a fixed bath or shower for every five sharing occupiers. In plain English, two general bathrooms are required in a house shared by between six and ten people where the bedrooms are not all en suite. For 11 to 15 there must be three general bathrooms, and so on. Further, where there are five or more occupiers of an HMO, every unit of living accommodation must contain a wash hand basin with appropriate splash back.

- All baths, showers and wash hand basins in an HMO must be equipped with taps providing an adequate supply of cold and constant hot water. All bathrooms must be suitably and adequately heated and ventilated, and all bathrooms and toilets must be of an adequate size and layout and suitably located. All baths, toilets and wash hand basins must be fit for purpose.

- If there are not cooking facilities within every living unit, there must be a kitchen for general use, suitably located, suitably equipped and of suitable size. This means, at the very least, sinks with adequate supply of both hot and cold water, draining boards, facilities for cooking food, electrical sockets, worktops for the preparation of food, cupboards for the storage of food and cooking utensils, refrigerators with adequate freezer compartments or separate freezers, appropriate refuse disposal facilities, and appropriate extractor fans, fire blankets and fire doors.

- Except where there are four or fewer occupants, the manager must also ensure that his or her name, address and any telephone contact number is made available to each household in the HMO and that such details are clearly displayed in a prominent position in the HMO.

When it comes to management standards, licensed landlords have a duty to take reasonable steps to ensure that tenants are not causing problems within the boundaries of the property through anti-social behaviour. Local authorities may in some instances put conditions on licences concerned with anti-social behaviour.

Local housing authorities may use their own amenity standards if they are equal to or higher than the minimum standards. This means landlords should contact their local authorities to confirm the standards to be applied in their own areas.

In the case of properties with insufficient amenities for the number of tenants the landlord wishes to house, local authorities will include conditions within licences stipulating that the required extra amenities must be provided within a specific time. Alternatively they may grant licence for lower maximum numbers of occupants. In some instances they may even conclude that a licence cannot be granted until the condition and amenities within a property are improved.

Fire safety standards

HMO landlords have to ensure there are adequate fire precautions (including alarms, extinguishers and fire blankets) and fire escape routes. These must be well maintained and adequate for the number of residents and the size of the property.

- HMOs should be fitted with fire warning systems such as fire alarms and heat or smoke detectors. These should be placed throughout the building but particularly in escape routes and areas of high risk, such as kitchens. The fire warning system should be serviced and checked regularly.

- Equipment such as extinguishers and fire blankets should be provided. There should be at least one fire extinguisher on each floor and a fire blanket in every kichen. These have to be checked periodically and the correct sort of extinguisher must be provided.

- HMOs should have an escape route that can resist fire, smoke and fumes long enough for everyone to leave (usually at least 30 minutes). This could be an external fire escape, or internal stairs, corridors or walkways that are specially constructed or treated to resist fire. All the walls, ceilings, floors and

❝HMO landlords have to ensure there are adequate fire precautions (including alarms, extinguishers and fire blankets) and fire escape routes. ❞

partitions along the escape route must be fire resistant. All the doors leading to the escape route must be fire resistant and must close automatically.

Occupier duties

The regulations also impose duties on the occupiers of HMOs, requiring them not hinder the manager (the landlord or his nominated representative) in the performance of his or her duties, to allow reasonable access to enable those duties to be performed, to provide information that is reasonably required for the purpose of carrying out those duties, and to take reasonable care to avoid causing damage to anything which the manager is under a duty to supply, maintain or repair.

Further, occupiers must store and dispose of litter in accordance with the arrangements made by the manager, and comply with his or her reasonable instructions in respect of any means of escape from fire, the prevention of fire and the use of fire equipment.

Applying for a licence

Landlords should check with their local authority for details of local requirements and HMO licensing arrangements. If a licence is required, it is to the local authority that an application should be made. Landlords are also required to inform *relevant persons* – primarily tenants and any other people with ownership interests in the freehold or leases associated with the building, the mortgage lender and, if using a letting agent or other firm to manage the let, the proposed managing agent – that an application has been made.

Following an application, the local authority may or may not inspect the building – it can choose to do so at any time within the licensing period. But either way it is required to satisfy itself within five years of receiving the application that there are no health or safety hazards in the building.

According to the government booklet 'Licensing of Houses in Multiple Occupation in England: A guide for landlords and managers', when considering licence applications local authorities must look at the following:

- the suitability of the HMO for the number of proposed occupiers

- the suitability of the facilities within the HMO, such as toilets, bathrooms and cooking facilities

- the suitability of the landlord and/or the managing agent to manage the HMO (*the fit and proper person test*)

- the general suitability of managing arrangements.

The local authority must also be satisfied that the licence holder is the most appropriate person to hold the licence.

Fit and proper person

The landlord might be thought unsuitable to hold the licence if he or she fails the *fit and proper person test*. This failure can arise if he or she has criminal convictions or has acted in a way that would indicate his or her unsuitability to manage this type of residential accommodation, for example because he or she has evicted a tenant unlawfully from a previous let, or has properties in which the council has had to step in to make emergency repairs.

Conditions of licences

Conditions attached to licences will include obtaining an annual gas safety certificate, keeping landlord-supplied electrical appliances and furniture in a safe condition (and providing declarations to this effect on demand), installing smoke alarms and keeping them in proper working order, and providing occupiers with statements of the terms on which they occupy the HMO. Landlords must also provide, on demand, declarations that they have complied with requirements concerning electrical appliances, furniture and smoke alarms.

Local authorities may also impose other conditions they deem necessary, such as conditions about the management of the HMO.

Before issuing a licence local authorities must send the applicant and *relevant persons* (primarily tenants and any other people with ownership interests in the freehold or leases associated with the building, the mortgage lender and the proposed managing agent) a copy of the proposed licence together with its reasons for the proposal. It must then consider any responses made by the applicant or those *relevant persons* before issuing the licence. After the licence has been issued, applicants also have a right of appeal against any conditions that have been attached to it – although not against the mandatory conditions concerning gas safety, the safety of electrical appliances and furniture, the installation of smoke alarms, and the provision of statements to tenants.

Licences are granted for a maximum of five years and there will be a fee to pay – this will vary from local authority to local authority ranging from zero to several hundred pounds.

Licences are only refused if there are serious difficulties concerning the HMO property, its proposed management or the fitness of those proposed to be involved in its management

Licences are not transferable. One must be obtained for each HMO property, and when one is sold or transferred, the new owner will have to arrange for a new licence application to be made for that building.

Planning permission (2010 changes)

Just prior to the 2010 general election, the British government made a change to planning law in England (not Wales or

Scotland), introducing a new specific use class for HMOs. As from 6 April 2010, any residential property let to three or more unrelated sharers, forming two or more households, were classed in planning law as HMOs. ('The Town and Country Planning (Use Classes) (Amendment) (England) Order 2010' can be downloaded from **www.opsi.gov.uk**).

According to a government briefing on the change, existing HMOs would not require planning permission to continue as before, even if the property were let to new tenants after April 2010. However, the onus would be on landlords to prove that their property had previously been used as a shared house – not on a local authority to prove that it was not (meaning HMO landlords would be advised to retain any evidence, such as letting records, so as to be able to answer challenges about past use).

For any property not formerly used as an HMO, after April 2010 it became a requirement that planning permission be obtained if the property was to be offered to let to three or more unrelated tenants forming two or more households – since this would now constitute a material change of use to a property. Larger HMOs – having more than six tenants – still do not have a category of their own but are likely to require planning permission in due course.

Reversion of a small HMO back into use as a family home (one used by one household) would be a permitted development and should not require planning permission, said the government. Landlords who rent to three to six unrelated sharers (from April 2010 classed as a C4 House in Multiple Occupation) have the right to revert the property to a family home (C3 Dwelling House) without requiring planning permission. However, landlords who let a shared house to a single person or family could, under the new regime, lose the right to let the property as an HMO without first obtaining new planning permission.

The change brought the planning law definition of an HMO into line with that within the Housing Act 2004.

The bottom line?

A government impact paper estimated the average cost to landlords of this change at between 2.5% and 5% of total rental income for one year. These costs include fees and administrative costs – planning application fees are put at £335, for example. It also admitted the change could reduce flexibility in the privately rented sector. Houses of the size often used as HMOs – generally three to four bedrooms – are often part of a landlord's rental portfolio without a particular type of occupancy in mind. In some cases the same property will be let to a family for a term and then individuals for the next term, falling back to a family after that.

The change brought a wave of protests from landlord representatives. And, come a change of government, these protests did not fall on deaf ears.

Revisions

In June 2010 the new Housing Minister Grant Shapps announced that he would be changing the planning rules further, saying he intended to allow changes of use between family houses and small, shared houses to take place freely without the need for planning applications. The following proviso was made:

"However, in those areas experiencing problems with uncontrolled HMO development, local authorities will be able to use their existing direction-making powers to restrict this freedom of movement by requiring planning applications. This change will allow the free development of smaller shared housing, which is a vital component of our private rented sector, unless there is a serious threat to the area."

The minister said his intention was to have revised rules in place by 1 October 2010.

Given the turnaround and the scope for confusion, not to mention the likelihood that different councils will interpret their powers in different ways, landlords should be sure to check with their own local planning authority when planning to let a property as an HMO if it has not been let to unrelated sharers before.

Taking responsibilities seriously

Landlords who do not take their fire safety responsibilities seriously enough can find themselves in serious trouble – as is the case with Norwich landlord Michael Billings.

Believed to be the landlord with the most rental properties in the East Anglian city, he was jailed in May 2010 after one of his bedsit tenants suffered near fatal burns.

Billings was not responsible for the fire that left his 19-year-old tenant Layla Skalli with 80% burns and fighting for her life (fire investigators thought it most likely the fire had started near an electricity meter). But he was responsible for not making sure his property had even basic fire protections such as working fire alarms, an adequate number of fire doors, or an adequate fire escape route.

When fire broke out, Skalli was marooned in her room above a shop in Norwich, cut off by smoke and unable to open her window more than a few inches. Firemen had to smash through the window to rescue her.

Billings admitted breaching the Health and Safety at Work Act, as well as gas and fire safety regulations; he was jailed for two and a half years and ordered to pay £20,000 costs. His jail sentence was later reduced to 21 months after he paid Skalli a further £20,000 by way of voluntary compensation as an expression of remorse.

Billings also admitted previous breaches of fire and safety regulations but his counsel told the court he had been refurbishing and upgrading his properties. He has since completed the work.

The charges were brought by both the Health and Safety Executive (HSE) and Norfolk Fire & Rescue Service. HSE Inspector John Claxton said Billings had failed in his basic duties as a landlord and those failures nearly cost the life of a young woman:

"Landlords have duties under law to maintain their properties and ensure they are safe places for their tenants to live. Michael Billings ignored these duties."

* * *

Section 3(2) of the Health and Safety at Work etc. Act 1974, under which Billings was charged, says:

"It shall be the duty of every self-employed person to conduct his undertaking in such a way as to ensure, so far as is reasonably practicable, that he and other persons (not being his employees) who may be affected thereby are not thereby exposed to risks to their health and safety."

Regulation 36 (3) (a) of the Gas Safety (Installation and Use) Regulations 1998 states:

"A landlord shall ensure that each appliance and flue … is checked for safety within 12 months of being installed and at intervals of not more than 12 months since it was last checked for safety."

Article 32(1) (a) of the Regulatory Reform (Fire Safety) Orders 2005 makes it an offence:

"for any reasonable person … to fail to comply with any requirement or prohibition imposed by regulations made, or having effect as if made … where that failure places one or more relevant persons at risk of death or serious injury in case of fire."

A full guide to landlords' duties can be downloaded from the HSE website at **www.hse.gov.uk**.

5.

Licences, Certificates and Safety Responsibilities

In England and Wales there is currently (June 2010) no general requirement for landlords to register or obtain a licence before letting their properties – and the coalition government has said it has no plans to change this. (Registration is required in Scotland, and will soon be required in Northern Ireland.)

However, even without registration, there are a number of requirements and duties that all landlords must adhere to – some applying only to specific types of property or specific geographical areas, and sometimes including the need for a licence.

These duties to protect tenants' safety are in addition to the more general ones that landlords have under the Health and Safety at Work etc Act 1974, the Management of Health and Safety at Work Regulations 1999, and Common Law.

Fire safety

The Regulatory Reform (Fire Safety) Order 2005, which applies to the common areas of houses in multiple occupation and of flats and maisonettes, requires appointment of a *responsible person* (a person who has control over the premises, for example, the manager or owner) who must conduct a fire risk assessment, paying particular attention to those at special risk, such as disabled people, those known to have special needs and children. The assessment should help identify risks that can be removed or reduced and to decide the nature and extent

❝ There are a number of requirements and duties that all landlords must adhere to. ❞

of the general fire precautions that are needed. General guidance on the regulations is included on the government website **www.communities.gov.uk**, from which the guidance booklet 'Fire

Safety Risk Assessment – Sleeping Accommodation', can be downloaded.

The responsible person is then charged with making such general fire precautions as may reasonably be required in the circumstances of the case to ensure that the premises are safe. There are also specialist firms that can fulfil these responsibilities on behalf of landlords.

HMOs are also covered by The Management of Houses in Multiple Occupation (England) Regulations 2006 (available from **www.opsi.gov.uk**). These require the person managing the HMO to ensure all measures are taken that are reasonably required to protect the occupiers from injury, having regard to the design of the HMO, its structural condition, and the number of occupiers. The manager must also ensure all means of escape from fires are kept free from obstruction, are maintained in good order and repair, and that any fire fighting equipment and fire alarms are maintained in good working order. Notices indicating the location of means of escape from fire must be displayed in positions within the HMO that enable them to be clearly visible to the occupiers.

Except where there are four or fewer occupants, the manager must ensure that his or her name, address and any telephone contact number are made available to each household in the HMO; and that such details are clearly displayed in a prominent position in the HMO. The regulations also impose duties on HMO managers to maintain water supply and drainage, to supply and maintain gas and electricity, and to maintain common parts, fixtures, fittings and appliances.

The regulations also impose duties on the occupiers of HMOs, requiring them to not hinder the manager in the performance of his or her duties, to allow reasonable access to enable those duties to be performed, to provide information that is reasonably required for the purpose of carrying out those duties, and to take reasonable care to avoid causing damage to anything which the manager is under a duty to supply, maintain or repair. Further, occupiers must store and dispose of litter in accordance with the arrangements made by the manager, and comply with his or her reasonable instructions in respect of any means of escape from fire, the prevention of fire and the use of fire equipment.

Fire safety guidance for landlords, explaining how to carry out fire risk assessments and keep residential buildings safe from fire has been published by LACORS, the Local Authorities Coordinators of Regulatory Services. 'Housing – Fire Safety' can be downloaded from the LACORS website **www.lacors.gov.uk**.

Gas safety

On moving in, every tenant must be provided with a gas safety certificate.

The Gas Safety (Installation and Use) Regulations 1998 require landlords to ensure gas fittings and flues are maintained in a safe condition and to have an annual safety check of appliances and flues carried out by a Gas Safe-registered engineer (information about the Gas safe Register, which replaced the Corgi Register in April 2009, can be found at **www.gassaferegister.co.uk**).

Landlords must retain a record of each safety check for at least two years. They must also provide a copy of the latest safety check record to existing tenants within 28 days of the check being completed, or to any new tenant before they move in.

Landlords who use managing agents should make sure the management contract clearly identifies who is to make arrangements for maintenance and safety checks to be carried out and who is to maintain the required records.

The Health and Safety Executive's booklet, 'Landlords: A guide to landlords' duties: Gas Safety (Installation and Use) Regulations 1998', can be downloaded from the HSE website at **www.hse.gov.uk**.

Electrical safety

Although there is currently no requirement in law for electrical installations and equipment to be inspected annually and certified as safe, the Electrical Equipment (Safety) Regulations 1994 (available from **www.opsi.gov.uk**) nevertheless require that electrical appliances supplied by landlords be safe to use at the start of each let.

Some voluntary landlord accreditation schemes do require inspections.

NICEIC[2], the electrical contracting industry's independent voluntary body (**www.niceic.org.uk** for the NICEIC's Landlords' fact sheet) advises landlords to have property maintenance and appliance testing procedures in place. Property should be inspected and tested by a competent person on change of occupancy, or at least every ten years – more often for higher risk properties, such as those where the installation is very old, or where damage has been found in the past. Appliances, cables, extension leads and electrical plugs should be inspected at the start of each tenancy for signs of wear and damage that could make them unsafe. Where there is reason to suspect that equipment is faulty, it should be tested.

Part P of the Building Regulations for England and Wales applies when electrical work is carried out in rental properties (similar rules apply in Scotland). In most cases this simply means that such work must be carried out, inspected and certified by a person registered with a government-authorised competent person scheme such as NICEIC. Alternatively, the relevant local building control must be notified prior to commencement of the work. Failure to comply with Part P is a criminal offence and local authorities have the power to require the removal or alteration of work that does not comply with the regulations.

---

[2] National Inspection Council for Electrical Installation Contractors.

Energy performance certificates

Landlords offering self-contained property for rent are required by law to provide prospective tenants with Energy Performance Certificates (EPCs) for properties about which they enquire.

EPCs provide an energy performance rating from 'A' (highly efficient) to 'G' (least efficient). The idea is that tenants are able to compare the energy efficiency of rental properties. Ratings are influenced by type of property, its age, layout, construction, heating, lighting and insulation. The typical rating for a property is D or E.

The certificates must be provided free either when (or before) any written information about the property is provided to prospective tenants or a viewing is conducted. They do not have to be provided if the landlord believes the prospective tenant is unlikely to have sufficient funds to rent the property or is not genuinely interested in renting, or the landlord is unlikely to be prepared to rent the property to the prospective tenant.

Certificates can only be issued by accredited domestic energy assessors or certified home inspectors. Once a property has been given an EPC, it gets a unique number and is registered on a national database by the assessor. Landlords can download extra copies from **www.epcregister.com** using the report reference number.

A new certificate does not have to be obtained for each let since EPCs are valid for ten years.

The full requirements are included in the Energy Performance of Buildings (Certificates and Inspections) (England and Wales) Regulations 2007 (available from **www.opsi.gov.uk**). The requirement to provide energy performance certificates is unaffected by the 2010 government announcement that the requirement for Home Information Packs (HIPs) when selling residential properties is suspended.

In Scotland, the Single Survey (the equivalent to HIPs) also includes an energy report requirement.

Deposits

When a landlord or letting agent in England and Wales takes a deposit from a tenant entering into an assured shorthold tenancy (AST – the default type of agreement between tenants and landlords), that deposit must be protected in a government-authorised tenancy deposit scheme designed to make sure deposits are held securely and their return (or otherwise) is dealt with fairly for both landlord and tenant.

Previously assured shorthold tenancies were the default type of tenancies for all properties let for less than £25,000 a year. However, shortly after taking office, coalition Housing Minister Grant Shapps confirmed he would stand by previously announced plans to increase the upper rental limit for ASTs to £100,000 as of 1 October 2010. This is an important change, since all letting agreements for rents of between £25,000 and £100,000 will automatically become ASTs and deposit protection rules apply.

Deposit protection schemes

There are two types of deposit protection schemes available for landlords and letting agents: insurance-based schemes and custodial schemes.

The first requires payment of a fee to the authorised scheme organiser to effectively insure the sum involved (although the landlord or agent retains the actual deposit) – the amount of fee varies over time, between schemes, according to the size of the deposit, the number of deposits taken, and whether

> **❝** No matter what, landlords must, within 14 days of accepting a deposit, both protect the deposit and provide the tenant with details of how this has been achieved. **❞**

or not the landlord is a member of a landlords association. Taking the My Deposit example (see below), at the time of writing there was a £57.50 joining fee plus a fee for each deposit over £300 of £29.36.

The second type of deposit protection scheme (the custodial scheme) is free to use but requires that the deposit be handed over to the scheme for safe keeping. All schemes provide a free dispute resolution service – an important element since the requirement for deposit protection was introduced after claims that some tenants were having the return of their deposits unfairly withheld.

Landlords can choose to use whichever scheme suits them best. But no matter what, they must, within 14 days of accepting a deposit, both protect the deposit and provide the tenant with details of how this has been achieved. That information must include the name and contact details of the scheme used, the landlord or agent's contact details, how to apply for release of the deposit, an explanation of the purpose of the deposit, and what the tenant should do if there is a dispute.

The three authorised schemes are:

1. The Deposit Protection Service (**www.depositprotection.com**, telephone 0844 47 27 000). This is the only custodial deposit protection scheme. It is free to use and open to all landlords and letting agents. Landlords can register online while the scheme provides a template for the information to be provided to tenants.

2. My Deposits, run by Tenancy Deposit Solutions Ltd (**www.mydeposits.co.uk**, telephone 0844 980 02 90). They are an insurance-backed scheme jointly owned by the National Landlords Association and Hamilton Fraser Insurance.

3. TDS Limited, which stands for both Tenancy Deposit Scheme and The Dispute Service – the same organisation, (**www.thedisputeservice.co.uk**, telephone 0845 226 7837) is an insurance-backed scheme. Landlords can join online and access a range of related forms and documents.

It is important that landlords comply with the requirement to protect deposits since if they do not they can be ordered to repay the tenant three times the amount of the deposit.

For the leaflet 'Letting? Are you protecting your tenant's deposit?' go to **www.direct.gov.uk**.

In September 2009, Scottish Minister for Housing and Communities, Alex Neil, announced that a national scheme to safeguard rent deposits would also be introduced in Scotland. Draft regulations were promised for 2010.

Deposits – claimed and left behind

George Watson was a new landlord who abided by all the rules.

He'd checked with the council that the two-bedroom terraced house he had inherited from his mother did not require a licence or planning permission before it could be let to a single family.

There was no mortgage, so no mortgage lender to be contacted.

He had had the gas appliances checked by a Gas Safe-registered engineer, and the electrical equipment checked by a NICEIC domestic installer, and had obtained an energy performance certificate. He had inspected the labels on the sofa and armchairs to make sure they were fire resistant, and he had smoke alarms fitted. He had even had the glass in an internal door replaced with safety glass. And he had new carpets fitted throughout and a new cooker put in.

When he took in his first tenants a couple of months later he had protected the £500 deposit via one of the two government-approved insurance based schemes. He thought there was nothing that could go wrong.

The couple who moved in were recommended by a family friend. A nice young couple, a bit down on their luck, he was told.

They turned out to be something of a nightmare. Although they paid the deposit and a month's rent in advance, after that they were always late with the rent. When George knocked, the door was never opened, and his text messages went unanswered.

In the fourth month he had to send a strongly worded letter threatening to bring proceedings if they did not bring the rent up to date. He also gave the couple notice to quit at the end of their six-month tenancy agreement. They continued to pay three weeks late.

After six months, much to George's relief, they moved out. He went into the house to clean up before new tenants moved in. Just a spruce up, he thought.

What he found made his heart sink. The place was filthy, there were stains on the carpets, holes in the walls where pictures had been nailed and then ripped down. The cooker was caked with grime and the door of the oven refused to close properly. The fridge had green things growing in it. Some plates and cutlery had gone missing. In the bedroom he found a selection of plastic and leather items whose use he could only guess at.

When the tenants asked for their deposit back, George refused. He reckoned that even keeping the £500 would leave him out of pocket.

But the tenants were not about to give up. They challenged George through the deposit protection scheme's dispute resolution arrangements. They claimed the house was dirty and the carpets were stained when they moved in; the cooker door had broken, but this was because it was faulty; and everything else was down to fair wear and tear.

George was flabbergasted. But when his claim was heard he had to admit he had very little evidence of the condition of the property on the day the tenants moved in. He had an inventory which they had signed, but this was not comprehensive and had nothing about the condition of the contents. Neither had he checked the tenants out. So he had only discovered the damage and missing items after they had left.

In the end his tenants got £350 of their £500 deposit back.

* * *

George, naturally, felt hard done by. But he resolved to treat the setback as a lesson. The next time tenants moved in he had them sign a fuller inventory. Also, he took a video of each room in the house, videoing the floors, the walls, soft furnishings and other furniture in detail. He didn't have problems with his new tenants – given the number of credit checks and references he had insisted on, the number of documents he had inspected and the questions he had asked it was hardly surprising (see next chapter) – and he was pleased to pay them back their deposit in full when they moved on 18 months later. But had there been a dispute, and a similar need to withhold the deposit as before, this time he would have been ready with sufficient evidence to back his claim.

The requirement for landlords to protect tenancy deposits was introduced in 2007 after a campaign by Citizens Advice and others claiming that landlords were unfairly withholding deposits at the end of tenancies. There are claims that despite the severe penalties for not protecting deposits, many landlords still fail to comply with the law when it comes to deposits. This clearly is not an acceptable or very clever way for landlords to go about their business, but without more research it is hard to tell how many of these are legitimate grievances and how many are misunderstandings or, as with George Watson, worse. It is probably a mixture of the three.

However, landlords who keep proper evidence of the contents of their properties and their condition when tenants move in and out (as George belatedly did), have little to fear. True, most disputes end in a split award between landlord and tenant but, according to Tenancy Deposit Solutions, 99.4% of deposits are returned without problems. And it reported, in March 2010, that landlords were currently being awarded part or all of disputed amounts in 51% of cases, with 43% split with the tenant and 8% awarded in full to the landlord.

"The more equitable balance between tenant and landlord has come about because landlords have improved the quality of the evidence they are providing to substantiate claims," said chief executive Eddie Hooker. "The law starts with the principle that the money is the tenant's. It's up to the landlord to justify withholding all or part of a deposit."

In October 2009 the same company reported that more landlords were turning to video footage as an effective way of proving a property's condition at the beginning and end of tenancy.

Meanwhile, in March 2010 The Deposit Protection Service reported it had discovered that tenants were leaving behind an array of possessions when moving out of their rented properties. Top of the list were sex toys, including pornographic magazines, raunchy underwear, bondage equipment and blow up dolls. Landlords also had to dispose of animals, both dead and alive, and in one instance the engine from a lorry. Other items left behind included the ashes of a dead person, a crash test dummy and a pair of synthetic breasts.

Mandatory HMO licensing

Since July 2006 landlords in England and Wales who own larger houses in multiple occupation have had to apply for licences from their local councils. If they do not do so they could find themselves fined up to £20,000 and unable to collect their rents.

There are three prongs to the HMO licensing process; two involving landlords themselves. First local authorities assess whether applicants are *fit and proper* to be HMO landlords and must satisfy themselves about the management standards they will apply. Later, or in some cases more immediately, come inspections to ratify landlord statements that their properties are fit for purpose. As licences state the maximum number of people each property may house, this includes an assessment of the suitability of amenities for the intended number of tenants.

When it comes to management standards, licensed landlords have a duty to take reasonable steps to ensure that tenants are not causing problems within the boundaries of the property through anti-social behaviour. Local authorities may in some instances put conditions on licences concerned with anti-social behaviour.

The Licensing and Management of Houses in Multiple Occupation and Other Houses (Miscellaneous Provisions) (England) Regulations 2006 (available via the website **www.opsi.gov.uk**) specified minimum amenity standards, setting out the requirements for kitchens, bathrooms and toilets in HMOs (see Houses in multiple occupation, above). Local housing authorities may use their own amenity standards if they are equal to or higher than the minimum standards. This means landlords should contact their local authorities to confirm the standards to be applied in their own areas.

In the case of properties with insufficient amenities for the number of tenants the landlord wishes to house, local authorities will include conditions within licences stipulating that the required extra amenities must be provided within a specific time.

Alternatively they may grant licence for lower maximum numbers of occupants. In some instances they may even conclude that a licence cannot be granted until the condition and amenities within a property are improved.

Selective licensing

Selective licensing laws, also introduced by the Housing Act 2004, allow councils to obtain powers to require licensing of all rental properties in specified areas. These are areas where they make a case that selective licensing powers are necessary to improve poor private rented sector standards.

To gain approval for such a licensing scheme, local authorities must demonstrate that the area covered has low housing demand (or is likely to become such an area) with a significant stock of privately owned houses let on short-term arrangements, or the area is experiencing a significant and persistent problem caused by anti-social behaviour and some or all private sector landlords in the area are not taking appropriate action to combat the problem.

Local authorities must show that a licensing scheme would fit in with their overall strategic approach to tackling problems in the local private rented sector, including existing policies on homelessness, empty properties, regeneration and anti-social behaviour. Before selective licensing can be introduced, local authorities must conduct a full and comprehensive consultation with local landlords, managing agents, tenants, residents and businesses on their proposals prior to submitting them.

A growing number of local authorities have sought and obtained selective licensing powers.

Licence terms

As in mandatory licensing, licences will only be issued to *fit and proper* landlords – which means taking into account any previous convictions relating to violence, sexual offences, drugs or fraud, and previous contraventions of laws relating to housing or landlord and tenant issues, and whether the applicant has been found guilty of unlawful discrimination practices.

Licences may include conditions relating to the management, use and occupation of the house. They must contain conditions requiring landlords to provide the local authority with an annual gas safety certificate, requiring electrical appliances and furniture supplied under the tenancy to be kept in a safe condition, smoke alarms kept in proper working order, requiring that occupiers be provided with written statements of the terms of occupation, and that references be required from anybody wishing to occupy the house.

* * *

As with mandatory licences, failure to obtain a selective licence can lead to a criminal conviction with a fine of up to £20,000 and will prevent the landlord taking any action in the courts to regain possession of the property should he wish to evict a tenant.

A copy of the fact-sheet 'Selective licensing of other residential accommodation' can be downloaded from the website **www.communities.gov.uk**. The booklet 'Landlords: Do you need a property licence?' can be downloaded from the same website.

Scotland

In Scotland, the first of the home countries to introduce a licensing scheme for HMO properties, it is now the law that, subject to a few exemptions, anybody who owns *any* residential property which is let must apply to register with the local authority for the area where the property is located. Examples of properties that are exempted are those which are also the landlord's only or main residence and in which there are not more than two lodgers, or those let only to members of the landlord's family. (More details are available on the website **www.landlordregistrationscotland.gov.uk**.) Landlords must register whether or not they use an agent. However, if they do use an agent they must disclose this and also the name of the agent, and both landlord and agent must be assessed (there is a fee for each) before an application can be approved. Agents have the option to register in their own names, which, if they manage more than two properties, makes the process easier and cheaper for their landlord clients.

Details of registered landlords, agents and properties are available on a central register published on the website **www.landlordregistrationscotland.gov.uk**. The register includes licensed HMO properties, which are entered automatically.

Northern Ireland

In March 2010, Northern Ireland's Social Development Minister, Margaret Ritchie, announced plans to introduce mandatory landlord registration to the province. A tenancy deposit protection scheme is to be introduced at the same time, along with an education and awareness programme for landlords and tenants and an *enhancement* of fitness standards for private rented properties.

The plans, expected to become law in Spring 2011, arise from consultation on a new private rented strategy: 'Building Sound Foundations'. Details are available on the website **www.dsdni.gov.uk**.

6.

Suitable Tenants

Once a suitable property has been acquired and necessary licences and certificates are in place, landlords are faced with finding suitable tenants. They should not accept anybody without first making adequate checks. After all, landlords entrust their tenants with valuable assets and although they can regain possession of their properties if things go wrong, this will take time – during which careless or malicious tenants can cause considerable damage both to their landlords' property and to his or her bank balance.

Landlords will want to know that prospective tenants are who they say they are, are in a position to pay the rent, and do not have a record of anti-social behaviour, mistreating property or ignoring their financial responsibilities.

Doing it Yourself

Finding tenants

Properties to rent can be advertised in the local press, various websites (for example, **www.simple2rent.co.uk**), or even in shop windows or supermarket message boards. Other possibilities are via local universities and any linked accreditation scheme or by direct contact with major employers.

Some housing associations and local authorities operate letting schemes. These tend to offer slightly lower rent levels than can be achieved on the open market, but are for a number of years – thereby removing the worry of void periods. The schemes take over management of rental properties and guarantee to return them to the landlord in good order at the end of the contracted period. Landlords who find this an attractive proposition and who are unlikely to want their properties back within two or three years should find out whether any such schemes run locally.

Some landlords simply prefer to have letting agents find their tenants. There are advantages and disadvantages – including the cost (see the section on letting agents later in the chapter).

Advertisement preparation

When advertising, it is important to remember which tenant group you are targeting and to match the publication's readership or, in the case of a website, visitorship profile, to the target group. This information should be freely available on associated websites and from sales representatives. This way you will not end up paying for wasted circulation to people unlikely or unable to rent your property, or who you would not want to rent to anyway.

Again some research into who is advertising what rental property, where, may save wasted time and money – as will research into the level of rents being advertised and, if relevant to the end of the market you are targeting, the level of local housing allowance. Clearly you need to pitch your rent at a level which is commercially acceptable to you, but not so high as make the property untenable for most would-be tenants in your preferred target group.

If you place an advertisement you should take care to make sure this is not discriminatory in any way – it is against the law to discriminate against potential tenants on the grounds of race, sex, disability, sexuality, or religion or belief. Besides basic information (such as number of bedrooms, parking arrangements and rent), your advertisement should be certain to mention any attributes your initial research identified as being particularly attractive to your target group (for example; 'good schools nearby', 'close to main-line railway station', 'in the heart of the city').

Handling responses

Once you have responses you will need to decide how you will treat prospective tenants and in what order. You will certainly need to arrange viewings, to ask tenants to complete an application form (even if there is only one applicant you will need to keep information provided by the tenant in case things go wrong), and to interview prospective tenants and seek references.

As you will be holding personal data, you should consider whether you need to register with the Information Commissioner's Office (**www.ico.gov.uk**). In any case you will need permission from those from whom you collect information if you intend to pass on any or all to others – for example, to undertake credit checks. You should do this by including a paragraph in the application form to be signed by the prospective tenant (see 'Questions to ask' on page 72).

Once you have personal information, you will have to make sure it is secure and that it is destroyed as soon as no longer required – say a month or two after a tenancy has ended and no outstanding issues remain.

Care should be taken to ensure questionnaire and interview questions are not in any way discriminatory or of such a nature that they could be construed as discriminatory. For example, landlords should not ask whether prospective tenants have a disability or illness, ask to see their medical records, or inquire as to their religion or place of birth.

But landlords are entitled to ask about ability to pay the rent and previous renting experiences.

Certainly do not ever agree to a tenancy before you have completed proper tenant checks, and never hand over keys or allow tenants to move in until you have made these checks, have a signed tenancy agreement and have received the first payment.

Questions to ask

The information you should seek from prospective tenants is as follows:

- Full name or names – you will need this, amongst other things, when making credit checks, or if you should need to trace the whereabouts of the person at a later date.

- Current address, telephone number(s) and email address – so you can contact them, and also so that you can make proper credit checks.

- How long he, she or they have been at their current address.

- If at the previous address less than 12 months, the two previous addresses, with dates – this is needed for effective credit checks.

- Whether the tenant or tenants are currently employed, unemployment, self-employed or in full-time education.

- If employed, the name, address and telephone number of the employer, job title, number of years employed, and National Insurance number – so you can seek a reference and, if things go wrong, have a point of contact and perhaps a means of recovering owed amounts by seeking an attachment on earnings.

- The name, address and other contact details of next of kin – this may be needed in emergencies but is also useful should you need to trace the tenant or tenants at a later date.

- Whether currently a home owner, in rented accommodation, living at home or with friends – useful in assessing financial risk.

- If in rented accommodation, the name, address and telephone number of the current landlord – so you can seek a reference.

- Whether single, married or living with a partner, and whether there are any children who will be living with the tenant or tenants.

- How many people in total will be living in the rental property and their relationship – important to know in case this would make a difference to the status of the property as an HMO or otherwise. Also, a declaration now can prevent arguments later on.

- Will there be any pets, and if so, what kind these are – some landlords prefer tenants not to have pets since they can increase the wear and tear on the property and its contents.

- Whether the prospective tenant or tenants is/are a smoker or non-smoker – again some landlords prefer non-smokers.

- Whether the prospective tenant or tenants have any County Court judgements (CCJs). CCJs affect credit rating and are usually considered an indication of increased financial risk.

- Whether he, she or they have ever been made bankrupt or been subject to any insolvency arrangements or agreements – again it would be an indication of increased risk that rents might not be paid if the answer is 'yes'.

- Whether the prospective tenant or tenants have ever been evicted from rented accommodation for any reason, and, if yes, what that reason was – if for non-payment of rent, or for causing damage, or for anti-social behaviour, the landlord would have cause to think twice.

- Whether the prospective tenant or tenants will be claiming local housing allowance (see the section later in the chapter).

- Whether a guarantor can be provided, and if so who that person is and how can he or she be contacted – landlords who consider accepting a guarantor as a way of reducing their financial exposure should also, after seeking their permission, conduct a credit check on anybody proposing to stand as guarantor.

- The names and addresses of at least two referees, including, if appropriate, the current landlord.

Of course, dishonest tenants may try to deceive landlords by giving untruthful answers, which is why the application form should be regarded as a starting point for the selection and verification process. Various of the answers given can be verified by different means – for example, employer details can be confirmed by contacting the employer, other details by a credit check.

Having the information on file is also important for another reason. If it later transpires that a tenant has given false information, this also provides grounds for seeking possession (the technical term for eviction, when the landlord takes back possession of his or her property) – see below, 'Ground 17: The landlord was persuaded to grant the tenancy on the basis of a false statement knowingly or recklessly made by the tenant, or a person acting at the tenant's instigation'.

It is well to remind prospective tenants of this on the face of the application form with some statement such as: 'Knowingly or recklessly making false statements to a landlord in order to obtain a tenancy are legal grounds for ending that tenancy.'

The application form should also contain a statement to be signed by the prospective tenant confirming that the information provided is correct and authorising the landlord to conduct credit checks and to seek references.

Interviews

Having obtained application forms and conducted viewings, landlords should interview those prospective tenants who have expressed an interest in renting. Besides confirming information included on the questionnaire, landlords can probe further about job security, previous renting experiences, ability to pay the rent, and the length of time the tenant is likely to wish to stay. Interviews can also be used to emphasise the landlord's attitude towards such things as pets, and to remind tenants that landlord insurance does not generally cover tenants' contents.

It is always better for the landlord to meet tenants in person before agreeing to rent to them, so this is a good opportunity. Interviews can be wrapped up with a visit to the rental property to go over any points about which the prospective tenants are uncertain. They do not need to be overly formal, but the landlord should take notes of what is said. If anything of significance is revealed or promised – such as the tenant agreeing to cut the grass every week and keep the flowerbeds in good order, or not to keep pets – this can be repeated in the letter letting the tenants know they have been accepted ('I am pleased to tell you, that having met you and conducted relevant credit checks, and upon your assurance that …').

Identity and credit checks

On this occasion or on a later date, but certainly before a tenancy agreement is signed, landlords should ask for sight of documents confirming prospective tenants' identity. Generally two or more of the following should be examined: a passport or driving licence (with picture), bank statement, utility, tax or similar bill showing current address, a wage slip bearing the name of the employer, the prospective tenant, and the NI number that has been declared on the application form. A note should be taken of relevant identification and account numbers.

A credit check should also be undertaken. As these will cost the landlord something (although not a great deal) they can usually be put off until the most likely prospective tenant has been identified. There are a number of suppliers who can be found with a simple internet search – such major players in the market as Experian, or more specialist companies such as Credit Check Services (which will also undertake tenant referencing). Different levels of report are typically offered, with higher level (and more expensive) reports offering more information.

Identity and credit checks can:

- pick up county court judgments against tenants

- report details of any bankruptcies

- confirm if the tenant is entered onto the electoral roll at the previous address and for how long he or she has been registered at that address

- provide a credit rating.

Tenants should be asked to explain any discrepancies between the credit check information and their application form answers.

References

Landlords should also take up references. These need to be treated with care, however, since some referees will feel constrained by personal relationship, fear of making themselves liable in some way, or even by ulterior motives – a current landlord who is keen to get rid of a tenant may steer clear of giving a bad reference, even if justified. And in any case, a prospective tenant is unlikely to give the name of somebody he or she knows will give a bad reference.

Banks will be very restrained in their answers and will generally only confirm, without liability, that the person named in the request for a reference holds an account with the bank and that the account number, sort code and address are in accordance with its records.

Requests to individuals named as referees can ask them to explain how they know the prospective tenant and for how long they have done so; as well as whether, in their opinion, the person would make a trustworthy, reliable and responsible tenant who will honour his or her tenancy responsibilities.

Again, the prospective tenants should be asked to explain any apparent discrepancies between the statements of referees and the answers given in the application forms.

If concerned about the financial standing of prospective tenants, as mentioned earlier in the chapter landlords can request a guarantor. This is somebody who contracts themselves to stand in the place of the tenant should he or she default on payment. Guarantors can be pursued for payment in the same way as tenants. However, before accepting a guarantor, landlords should satisfy themselves of the identity and financial standing of the guarantor, just as they would a tenant – by a credit check and sight of documents confirming identity in the same way. Landlords should also be aware that the value of a guarantor who lives overseas is very limited since it will be difficult to pursue an overseas resident, even an EU resident, through the courts.

Avoid an identity crisis

People do falsify their identities and usually not for good purposes.

People who have bad credit records or criminal records to cover up, people who are illegal immigrants, or those who simply want to steal have all been known to adopt false identities. Any landlord taking on somebody of this ilk as a tenant is likely to have problems – so it is important to check the identity of would-be tenants with care.

But tenants and landlords can themselves be the victims of identity theft.

Tenants are particularly vulnerable if they fail to inform everybody they should of a change in their address and do not redirect their mail to their new home. Fraudsters can use utility bills, mobile phone bills, credit card bills, bank account details, correspondence from the Revenue and the like to obtain credit cards, or to bamboozle unsuspecting landlords.

Landlords who leave personal documents in their rented home, even if in a locked drawer in a locked room, or who allow mail to be sent to them at the rented property, can also find their tenants trying to steal their identities to buy goods or services, or even worse.

In 2005, Brighton landlord Grahame Hawthorn, who had been living overseas for the past seven years, effectively had both his identity and his house stolen by his tenant.

The tenant, going by the name of Andrew Manning, was introduced by a letting agent. He passed the checks that were made of his income, employment and identity. He paid six months' rent in advance plus a deposit of £1,200 – almost £7,000 in all.

In fact, he never moved in; he only went to the house to collect the mail, which included utility bills addressed to Grahame Hawthorn.

But a week after taking possession, having made a search on the Land Registry and found both that Grahame was the owner of the house and that there was no mortgage, Manning went to a financial adviser saying he wanted to take out a loan against the house. He told the financial adviser that his name was Grahame Hawthorn and that he wanted to borrow £294,500, roughly 90% of the then market value of the terraced home.

The broker asked for two forms of identification, which Manning duly provided, one in the form of a driving licence in the name of Grahame Hawthorn living at the Brighton address. He gave his employers as a bogus firm he had created. Its address and telephone number was that of a confidential accommodation address and personalised answering service he had paid for. He gave false income figures.

The financial adviser wrote to the firm and of course received confirmation of Manning's employment and salary – in a letter almost certainly written by Manning himself, using a different name.

> **❝** Landlords who leave personal documents in their rented home, even if in a locked drawer in a locked room, or who allow mail to be sent to them at the rented property, can find their tenants trying to steal their identities to buy goods or services, or even worse. **❞**

A first mortgage application made to Cheltenham & Gloucester was turned down. However, almost immediately Manning did obtain a mortgage from GMAC-RFC. He put the money in a bank account he had opened for the purpose, quickly withdrawing it and disappearing.

All this was only discovered when the letting agent, going to the house to prepare for a new rental, found an abandonment notice pinned to the door on the property.

GMAC-RFC, which had not received a single mortgage payment, had ordered the locks changed and local estate agents to sell the property.

However, when the truth was discovered, GMAC-RFC relented. It, and Grahame Hawthorn, had been the victim of a sophisticated fraud, it said. Grahame Hawthorn got his house back – but no doubt not without first suffering some weeks of anxiety.

Manning had been able to engineer the theft of over £200,000 using Grahame's identity even though the landlord was white, in his 50s and living abroad, while he was black and in his 30s and had even misspelt Grahame's name on some of the mortgage application documents.

Using an Agent

Some landlords prefer to appoint letting agents to find suitable tenants, often to provide a full letting service which includes collecting rents and dealing with tenant problems, including necessary repairs and the like. On the one hand, this provides convenience and, hopefully, know-how. On the other, it eats up some of the rental income and, unless due care is taken in appointing an agent and checking the agency agreement in some detail, it can prove risky – letting agents can and do go bankrupt or simply abscond leaving money owed to their landlord clients.

In law an agent acts on behalf of the principal (you) and can make binding agreements. But having an agent does not absolve a landlord of responsibility. So landlords should be extremely cautious about who they appoint as their agents.

The problem is that anybody can currently set themselves up as a letting agent – even if he or she has no proper training, no knowledge of the market, and no financial savvy. The Labour government of 2005-10 had put out proposals for licensing letting agents, but coalition Housing Minister Grant Shapps made plain in 2010 that he had no intention of following this through – so landlords should choose letting agents with great care.

Credentials

In particular they should look for firms that belong to professional bodies, with proper procedures in place for redress – for example, members of the Association of Residential Lettings Agents (**www.arla.co.uk**), which is linked to the National Association of Estate Agents (**www.naea.org.uk**), or the Royal Institution of Chartered Surveyors (**www.rics.org.uk**).

> **❛❛** A problem is that anybody can currently set themselves up as a letting agent. **❜❜**

The minimum that should be looked for is membership of the government-backed National Approved Letting Scheme (NALS – **www.nalscheme.co.uk**). Supported by ARLA, NAEA and RICS (Royal Institution of Chartered Surveyors), the NALS gives accreditation to letting and management agents that agree to meet defined standards of customer service, that have insurance cover to protect clients' money, and have a complaints procedure offering independent redress.

Membership is voluntary and letting agents signify membership by displaying the NALS logo in their premises and sometimes on their letterheads.

It is also wise to check that agents are registered with the Property Ombudsman's Scheme for Lettings. This is a government-backed scheme for dealing with maladministration. Member firms will have agreed to follow the Property Ombudsman's Code of Practice for Letting Agents and to allow the Ombudsman to resolve disputes referred by landlords or tenants and relating to lettings and management agents (details on **www.tpos.co.uk**).

> **❝ The minimum that should be looked for is membership of the government-backed National Approved Letting Scheme (NALS). ❞**

Formerly the Ombudsman for Estate Agents (OEA), the Property Ombudsman is charged with resolving disputes between property sales and letting agents who have joined the OEA scheme and their clients, including landlords. The service is free and independent.

The scheme is open to all those firms of estate agents with a principal, director or partner who is a member of the National Association of Estate Agents (NAEA) or Royal Institution of Chartered Surveyors (RICS); to all corporate estate agents, such as subsidiaries of banks, building societies and insurance companies or who are independently quoted on the Stock Exchange. It is also open to other estate agents who are sponsored and seconded by existing member agents.

Since October 2008, all estate agents have been required to register with an Estate Agents Redress Scheme, such as the OEA, that has been approved by the Office of Fair Trading (OFT) and which investigates complaints against estate agents.

Lettings and property management agents are not required to register in this way but may do so. When they join the OEA they also subscribe to the Code of Practice for Letting Agents.

ARLA claims to lead the industry in setting and regulating standards and in its demand that its members act with professionalism and commitment to customer service. Besides a Code of Practice, membership byelaws require compliance with such issues as handling, accounting for, and protecting clients' money, that members have professional indemnity insurance in place (meaning they are covered for awards against clients if they are ever found to have acted negligently), and have procedures for dealing with complaints. There are disciplinary procedures for those who transgress, when agents can be asked to account for their actions before their peers.

Besides checking that a letting agent is aligned with a professional body or is accredited by NALS, prudent landlords will check the financial standing of the firm before entering into any binding commitment. This might take the form of asking probing questions or requesting sight of accounts – limited companies must file accounts at Companies House (**www.companieshouse.gov.uk**) where they can be searched for a modest fee. There is also the option to obtain a credit check on the firm.

Contractual matters

Contracts offered by letting agents are binding and should be scrutinised carefully before signing. Any unwelcome or unclear clauses should be questioned. Terms and conditions, which will undoubtedly form part of or be referred to in the contract, should be requested in writing and should be read with the utmost care.

Landlords do not have to accept the contract that is presented to them and the terms can be varied by agreement before any document is signed.

Points to look out for include the following:

Services provided

These should be described in precise terms. If doing more than simply finding suitable tenants, a letting agent can take on a raft of responsibilities, including being the initial contact for tenants, dealing with minor maintenance and repairs issues, ensuring paperwork is correct, collecting and handing over rents, collecting and protecting deposits, taking an inventory of contents, and making regular inspection visits. Make sure the services detailed in the contract are those, and only those, that you wish the agent to perform. It is particularly important that it is clear who is responsible for obtaining and retaining gas safety certificates and for providing copies of these to tenants.

Fees

These are usually expressed as a percentage of the rental income over the letting term, and can range significantly from firm to firm, so it pays to shop around. It also pays to check if there are any additional charges that the agent can levy – for example, for tenancy agreements, setting up charges, or charges for taking and checking inventories.

Tenant vetting

According to the Property Ombudsman (**www.tpos.co.uk**), a major cause of disputes between landlords and agents is the quality of tenant referencing undertaken by agents. Landlords should check whether or not a referencing service is provided and the extent of checks made (are credit references obtained, employee references, previous landlord references, bank references and, if appropriate, guarantor references?). Tell the agent from the outset you want to know full tenant details, and receive a copy of the application form. Agents sometimes plead that data protection laws do not allow them to pass on such details. However, if authority is sought from the tenant at the outset, this is not the case.

Authorised expenditure

If the agent is to be given authority to undertake minor repairs and maintenance and to recoup this from rent received or to charge you directly, you will want some kind of monetary limit put upon this so you are not suddenly saddled with a large bill you previously knew nothing about.

❝ If the agent is to be given authority to undertake minor repairs and maintenance, you will want some kind of monetary limit put upon this. **❞**

Paperwork

Be sure it is made clear who is responsible for obtaining and retaining necessary certificates, registrations and licences (such as gas safety certificates, energy performance certificates, and HMO licences, if required), for maintaining records concerning utility services, council tax and the like, and for passing necessary information on to tenants. You should enquire about the form of tenancy agreement to be used (in most cases this will be an assured shorthold tenancy – see next chapter) and about the source of the wording (is this from a professional body template, for example, or has it been prepared by a solicitor?). Are there any optional clauses that have been added – for example, on pets – or are there any you would like added, such as responsibility for maintaining the garden?

Deposits

Tenancy deposits must be protected by law via one of the authorised deposit-protection schemes mentioned on page 57. You will need to know that the agent will deal with this, along with the protection scheme they will use, and that the agent will provide information about the scheme to incoming tenants.

Rent arrears

You should enquire as to the procedure for chasing overdue rent. Usually the agent will issue a written reminder, followed by a warning letter and, if necessary, possession procedures. At what point does each of these kick in? You will not want your rent to be allowed to run overdue by more than a week or two at the most, so reminders have to be issued within a few days of rent falling into arrears. You will want to know that you will be informed of any late payments and the action being taken.

Renewals

Some letting agents' contracts can be very hard to terminate. This can become an issue if the letting agent does no more than find a tenant who then stays at the property over a number of years. It could be that the contract requires you to pay the fee and/or commission all over again each time the tenant renews. In 2010, the Office of Fair Trading contested the fairness of at least one letting agent's terms. The National Landlords Association was also amongst those to complain about the practice. It is therefore best to be clear at the outset as to what it is you are agreeing to when it comes to termination and renewals.

Service levels

Ideally you would like to see service levels written into your contract so that the frequency of regular events – such as the payment to you of rent, or of property inspections – are specified and deadlines set for dealing with irregular events – such as being informed within, say, seven days, of repairs undertaken, or of notice being received, or undertaking to answer correspondence within seven days.

Letting agents who act for landlords who are resident overseas are obliged to deduct basic rate tax from the rent (tenants of non-resident landlords who do not have a UK letting agent acting for them are obliged to do the same if the rent is over £100 a week). The deduction is made after taking off deductible letting expenses, which included the agents' fees and other outgoings associated with the let, and is remitted to the Revenue.

There is a way for overseas landlords to get around this deduction of tax from their rent received. Landlords can make an application to the Revenue. Details of how to do this are on the Revenue website **www.hmrc.gov.uk** (search 'The Non-Resident Landlords (NRL) Scheme').

Many letting agents provide a good and helpful service to landlords. However, if things should go wrong, landlords should complain first to the agent concerned. If that does not bring a satisfactory response, the route is through the professional body concerned, or NALS, followed by the Property Ombudsman.

“ It is best to be clear at the outset as to what it is you are agreeing to when it comes to termination and renewals. **”**

There are letting agents and then there are letting agents

Complaints against letting agents are legion. Claims of poor service, failing to do what is promised, not making inspection visits, late payment, not taking out proper references, not protecting tenants' deposits, not responding to correspondence or calls, even renewing or taking on new tenants without the landlord's knowledge, are all complaints that feature on websites such as **www.residentiallandlord.co.uk** and landlord forums.

Just as landlords are unjustly sometimes all tarred with the same rogue label, so letting agents all suffer because of the poor performance of some. Even so, there is no doubt that there are a lot of landlords who have been disappointed by their letting agents. Often these are smaller letting agencies, of which there are an estimated 15,000 or so in the UK. Sometimes there is more than a whiff of sharp practice, as when agents try to charge year after year for a tenant they found years before, or whose contracts are hard to break.

The bottom line is that landlords have to be confident that they can trust their agents – after all, both the landlord's reputation and his or her rental income is at stake. Most especially, landlords have to be certain that the rent collected on their behalf will be paid over to them – and to do that they must check the credentials of any firm they appoint.

Even with checking, things do not always turn out as hoped.

For example, in 2006 the Office of Fair Trading (OFT) banned Hertfordshire letting agent Richard McCarthy, the owner of McCarthy Woods Ltd, from undertaking further estate agency work. The consumer protection body had taken action following McCarthy's conviction for fraudulent trading and failing to pass on rent that he had collected on behalf of landlords.

"Whether buying or letting a property, when consumers give money to an agent, it is essential that they can rely on the trustworthiness of that agent. If an agent engages in any form of fraudulent conduct, the OFT will not hesitate to take action to prevent them from working as an estate agent." said OFT director of consumer regulation enforcement, Christine Wade.

This was just one of a number of bans and warnings issued against letting agents by the Office of Fair Trading in recent years. It has also been active in monitoring lettings agents' terms and conditions and in some instances persuading them to make changes.

It famously took London letting agent Foxtons to court over its terms. In early 2009 the High Court ruled in its favour. Foxtons had until January 2010 to lodge an appeal but instead made changes to its terms and conditions.

The case was brought under the Unfair Terms in Consumer Contracts Regulations 1999. The High Court agreed that Foxtons' renewal commission terms were not transparent enough. It also ruled that terms in the Foxtons contract that required landlords to pay renewal commission even after the sale of their property should a tenant remain in occupation were unfair, not binding, and therefore could not be enforced by the firm. Likewise, similar terms that required landlords to pay sales commission to Foxtons in the event that a rental property was sold to a tenant introduced by Foxtons was ruled to be unfair.

The OFT said Foxtons had subsequently made significant changes to its standard landlord contract following its intervention. These changes included making the liability to pay renewal commission more transparent, reducing the commission payable on renewal, and limiting it to two renewals.

7.

Tenancy Agreements

Private renting, as the term implies, is a private agreement between a tenant and landlord. The rent payable, when it is payable, whether in advance or in arrears, whether a deposit is paid, whether furnishings are provided or not, are all matters to be agreed between tenant and landlord.

In England and Wales, unless the tenancy is to be for a fixed period in excess of three years, this agreement could be verbal – although this is inadvisable, since verbal agreements are often hard to enforce. Even if verbal, tenants whose assured shorthold tenancy started on or after 28 February 1997 have a right to ask for a written statement of the main terms of the tenancy, including:

- the date on which it began
- the amount of rent payable
- the dates on which it is due
- any rent review arrangements
- the length of any fixed term.

Certain information – about deposits, gas safety and energy performance – must in any case be provided by the landlord in writing.

Put it in writing

So, when agreeing to let a property to new tenants, prudent landlords should always draw up a written tenancy agreement.

You will not have complete *carte blanche* as to what is included. To some extent this is dictated by legislation, including the Housing Acts and the Unfair Terms in Consumer Contracts (Amendment) Regulations 2001 and by Office of Fair Trade guidance on unfair terms in tenancy agreements (**www.oft.gov.uk**).

> **❝** When agreeing to let a property to new tenants, prudent landlords should always draw up a written tenancy agreement. **❞**

The general rule is that the greater the number of restrictions and conditions that are placed on tenants and the more limitations put on landlord liability, then the greater the likelihood that the tenancy agreement will be open to challenge.

Legally it makes no difference whether the property is to be provided *furnished* or *unfurnished* or somewhere in between. The tenure, the right to occupy the property, will be the same.

Government advice ('Assured and Assured Shorthold Tenancies: A guide for landlords' – **www.communities.gov.uk**) is that landlords may draw up their own agreements, but, if they do so, they must make sure that the terms are fair and do not conflict with the duties imposed on landlords by legislation (which will automatically override anything included to the contrary). However, "if you do decide to draw up your own agreement you are strongly advised to seek legal advice. For this reason it may be better to use standard tenancy agreements".

Standard tenancy agreements are easy to obtain and are relatively cheap. For example, the website **www.tenancy-agreements.net** has agreements that can be downloaded in Word format, and edited to include landlord and tenant details and to include or exclude optional clauses.

* * *

The exact coverage and content of a tenancy agreement will, of course, depend in large part on the form of tenancy which your let(s) fall under. This chapter therefore firsts explains the various forms of tenancy in existence, before moving on to look in detail at suggested agreement content for the most common kind of tenancy in the buy-to-let market.

Types of Tenancy

Assured tenancies

Since the introduction of the Housing Act 1988, most new tenancies have been *assured tenancies*, and since the Housing Act 1996, most have been *assured shorthold tenancies* (ASTs), This means ASTs are the default form of agreement for most tenancies.

Assured tenancies were introduced to encourage development of the private rented sector by lifting restrictions on the rent that could be asked and by making it easier to regain possession of the property. The Housing Act 1996 went further by making it easier to set up assured shorthold tenancies and by introducing provisions intended to make it easier and quicker to evict tenants who have fallen behind with their rent or who cause nuisance.

The difference between the two types of tenancy is that assured shorthold tenancies allow landlords to bring tenancies to an end after six months (or on expiry of the fixed term, if longer) simply by giving two months' notice. Assured tenancies (rather than assured shorthold tenancies), give tenants greater security of tenure (section 21 of the Housing Act 1988 does not apply – see *Possession*, below) and are now used mostly in the social housing sector.

If, at the end of the term specified in the agreement, the tenancy is simply allowed to run on with no new tenancy agreement issued but the tenant remaining living in the property, the tenancy becomes a *periodic tenancy*. The same terms and conditions apply as in the original tenancy agreement, except that there is no minimum six-month period.

So in the case of a periodic tenancy arising out of an AST, the tenancy can be brought to an end by the landlord giving two months' notice (he or she does not have to wait another six months), or by the tenant or tenants giving one month's notice.

But in the case of an assured tenancy other than an assured shorthold tenancy, the term of the periodic tenancy will be the same as the original fixed-term tenancy – so if for one year, then for one year more.

However, if the need arises, there is provision for seeking a change in rent and other terms during an assured periodic tenancy. Section 6(2) of the Housing Act 1988 allows either the landlord or his or her tenant or tenants to apply, within 12 months of the original tenancy agreement expiring, for variation in the terms of the agreement with or without a consequential change in the rent. Section 13(2) of the act allows either the landlord or the tenant to apply annually for a change in the rent only.

In either case the notice must be served in the prescribed form (available from **www.communities.gov.uk**). If the party on whom the notice has been served chooses not to respond within the allowed period, the change becomes effective. However, should he, she or they object, they can appeal to a Rent Assessment Committee (again using the prescribed form) which will adjudicate the issue.

Unless stated otherwise, private sector tenancy agreements entered into since February 1997 are automatically assured shorthold tenancy agreements. But there are exceptions: holiday lets, where no rent or a very low rent is charged; where the rent is in excess of £25,000 (£100,000 from 1 October 2010); where the tenant is a company; or where the accommodation is shared with a resident landlord. For these exceptions, different types of agreement are needed – namely *common law* tenancy agreements which stand on their own merits outside the restrictions and protections of the Housing Acts.

* * *

Tenancies which cannot be assured or assured shorthold tenancies

The following tenancies cannot be assured or assured shorthold tenancies:

- a tenancy which began, or which was agreed, before 15 January 1989

- a tenancy for which the rent is more than £25,000 a year (£100,000 from 1 October 2010)

- a tenancy which is rent free or for which the rent is £250 or less a year (£1,000 or less in Greater London)

- a business tenancy or tenancy of licensed premises (where alcohol is sold or consumed)

- a tenancy of a property let with more than two acres of agricultural land or a tenancy of an agricultural holding

- a tenancy granted to a student by an educational body such as a university or college

- a holiday let

- a letting by a resident landlord (one who lives in the same property as his tenants)

- a tenancy where the property is owned by the Crown or a government department (however, lettings by the Crown Estate Commissioners, the Duchy of Cornwall or the Duchy of Lancaster may be assured tenancies)

- a tenancy where the landlord is a local authority, a new town, a development corporation, a housing action trust, or a fully mutual housing association.

Tenancies which can be assured but not assured shorthold tenancies

The following tenancies cannot be shorthold tenancies:

- a tenancy replacing an earlier assured tenancy with the same tenant which has come to an end or a statutory periodic tenancy arising automatically when the fixed term of an assured tenancy ends (in other words assured tenants who stay on cannot be made to accept a less secure tenure than they previously enjoyed)

- an assured tenancy which the tenant has succeeded to on the death of the previous regulated (pre-1989) tenant

- an assured tenancy following a secure tenancy as a result of the transfer of the tenancy from a public sector landlord to a private landlord

- an assured tenancy arising automatically when a long leasehold tenancy extending over a number of years expires.

Note that the £25,000 upper rent limit for ASTs no longer applies after 1 October 2010. From that date the limit is £100,000, the upward shift made to take account of inflation since the limit was first enacted and also to bring in student lets and the like where there is one agreement in place for the whole property, signed by all the tenants, and the aggregate rent exceeds £25,000.

Assured shorthold tenancies

As can be seen from the above, the form of tenancy agreement used will depend on the nature of the tenancy. However, in the vast majority of instances assured shorthold tenancy agreements (ASTs) will be the appropriate type of agreement to use. In simple terms, ASTs put landlords in the driving seat when it comes to ending tenancies. Although things can, and sometimes do, get messy and protracted, landlords should never have to wait more than a few months to regain possession of their properties even from the most delinquent and crafty tenants.

An AST can be for any period but, regardless of this, tenants have security of tenure for the first six months. During this time they can only be required to leave if they breach the terms of the agreement in such a way as to give grounds for possession (see 'Possession' below). After the expiry of six months, or at the expiry of the fixed term of the tenancy, if longer, landlords may require tenants to leave simply by giving two months' ('section 21') notice.

For this reason ASTs are most commonly for six month periods only. Tenants can then be asked to leave at the expiry of the six months. Alternatively, when the fixed term expires, the landlord may grant the tenants a further fixed term tenancy agreement, or simply allow them to stay on under the same terms. In such circumstances there is no need for additional paperwork; the tenancy simply becomes a *periodic tenancy*. Tenants can quit periodic tenancies by giving the landlord one month's notice and may be required to leave on receipt of two months' written notice.

Tenancy agreements provide landlords and tenants with both the express rights and obligations spelled out in the agreement (always provided these are not at odd with the Housing Acts – so for example, a landlord may not require tenants to give longer periods of notice than is laid down, or claim the right to give shorter notice that required by legislation) and with implied rights. The latter may or may not be referred to, but are included in statute or are common law rights.

So, for example, tenants are entitled to the *quiet enjoyment* of their home and landlords may not demand access without notice, or enter the premises when the tenants are not present. Landlords have a duty of care towards their tenants and tenants have a duty of care towards the property they are renting. Tenants have a right to know the name and address of their landlord and to know how their deposit has been protected if this information is not included in the tenancy agreement.

As in any legal agreement, tenancy agreements should set out the parties to the agreement, and the date on which the agreement is made. ASTs should also include the start date and duration of the tenancy, the amount and frequency of rental payments. If the tenancy is for more than six months, the AST can include break clauses and also agreed rental increases at specified future dates. Responsibilities for general outgoings (rates, utility bills, repairs and maintenance) and other responsibilities of the two parties should be recited.

Landlords have an opportunity to include restrictions that they deem necessary – for example a bar on redecoration without prior written consent from the landlord or restrictions on the number of people who may live or stay in the premises.

There may be peculiarities to the property, such as a right of way over part of the garden, which need to be specified.

It is also good practice to include clauses dealing with late payment of rent and also with the termination of the tenancy.

When it comes to late payment of rent, landlords can specify a (reasonable) rate of interest that may be charged on overdue amounts and also make tenants responsible for any debt collection costs should these arise because of late payment of rent.

Sometimes tenants leave possessions behind. Dealing with these can be a nuisance if nothing is said about them in advance. A reasonable condition would be to say that the landlord may remove and store any possessions left by a tenant for (say) 28 days after which he or she may, after giving the tenant due notice, dispose of them – the tenant remaining liable for reasonable removal, storage and disposal costs.

It is also reasonable to say that the premises must not be left unoccupied for more than, say, 21 days (or the maximum specified in the relevant insurance policy). The tenancy agreement can specify that if the property is left empty for any longer period the landlord will have reasonable cause to believe the tenant has abandoned the property when he or she may (even though the tenant has not given formal notice), treat the tenancy as ended and enter the premises.

Other possible restrictions include specifying that a particular room or area may not be used and is to be kept locked, requiring that tenants or their guests do not smoke indoors, or do not keep pets in the house. However, any clauses of this nature should not be so restrictive as to be unreasonable.

Common law tenancies

- For holiday lets, all that is needed is a simple agreement stating, among other things, that the rental is for a defined period and is for holiday accommodation only.

- Lodging agreements for rental of rooms in houses shared with landlords can amount to tenancies (in general terms if the tenant has exclusive use of a room) or a licence to lodge – see 'Letting rooms in your home: A guide for resident landlords', **www.communities.gov.uk**. Either way *lodgers* have fewer rights and less secure tenure than tenants who are party to assured or assured shorthold tenancy agreements.

- For low or high rents, and for company lets, a full tenancy agreement is needed setting out rights, duties and tenure in some detail.

As rights and duties are not covered by statute, common law tenants have, in general, less secure tenure than tenants with an assured or assured shorthold tenancy. However, this also means more needs to be spelled out in the agreement – such as what notice is required, who may live in the house, rights of (or restrictions on) assignment (passing on the agreement to a successor) and what happens if the lease expires but no notice is given (if nothing is said about the lease being renewed monthly it is likely to be deemed to have been renewed for the length of the original lease).

Deposit-protection requirements apply to assured shorthold tenancies only, so landlords of properties in England and Wales with common law tenancies need not cover the deposit in a government-approved scheme (see Licences, Certificates and Safety Responsibilities above). However, neither does the important 'section 21' possession procedure apply (gaining possession by simply giving notice).

Regulated tenancies

There are also still a number of *regulated tenancies* in place – in general these are a hangover from a former letting regime and are tenancies that began before January 1989 or new tenancies arising from regulated tenancies (for example, where the tenant has accepted alternative accommodation).

Regulated tenancies restrict the amounts by which landlords can increase rents – generally a *fair rent* set by a rent officer, with increases from thereon limited to inflation plus 5%. They also make landlords responsible for major repairs and give tenants and their heirs considerable security of tenure. Regulated tenancies can apply to all or part of a house, flat, maisonette or bungalow and can be furnished or unfurnished, but do not apply where there is a live-in landlord.

Evicting a tenant from a property which is the subject of a regulated tenancy is extremely difficult. The courts can only grant possession orders in limited circumstances. Further, if tenants die, their spouses (or somebody living with them as if husband or wife), will normally take over their regulated tenancy (another family member who has been living in the home for two years can also take over the tenancy but this will be an assured, not a regulated, tenancy).

When it comes to rent, either the landlord or the tenant can apply to the rent officer for a fair rent to be registered. Once that has been done, the registered rent is the maximum that can be charged until it is reviewed or cancelled on application to the rent officer. Even if a rent is not registered, the landlord can only increase the rent in certain circumstances.

Because the amount of rent that can be charged is restricted, because regulated tenants have security of tenure, and because they are often older and more resistant to changes and improvements being made to their homes, the capital value of properties with regulated tenancies are usually substantially lower than similar properties without tenants.

Possession problems

To free up property with regulated tenants for refurbishment or development, landlords sometimes try to use provisions which allow them to move regulated tenants to suitable alternative accommodation. The procedure requires court approval – which the court will only give if convinced it is reasonable to do so, and that alternative accommodation is of sufficient size and condition, and is presented with a certificate from the local council confirming that the alternative accommodation is indeed suitable. Should the move to alternative accommodation be approved, the new tenancy will also be a regulated tenancy.

❝ The capital value of properties with regulated tenancies are usually substantially lower than similar properties without tenants. ❞

Another ground for possession is that there is statutory overcrowding in the property, as defined in the Housing Act 1985.

Statutory overcrowding has a fairly complicated definition which boils down to a requirement that each resident should have a reasonable amount of sleeping accommodation, and that unrelated adults of the opposite sex do not have to share the same room. Children under ten may share a room with anybody of the opposite sex. How many same sex people should be permitted to sleep in the same room is determined by floor area – at least 70 square feet for one person, 110 square feet for two people. Rooms counted as sleeping accommodation include living rooms, dining rooms, bedrooms and the living area of an open-plan kitchen/living room. As a general rule, one room is considered suitable for one or two people, if the two people are of the same sex or are partners, or one or both are aged under 10. Two rooms are considered suitable for up to three people, and three rooms for up to five people.

In addition, the HHSRS, which applies to all residential properties (see earlier), includes "crowding and space" as one of its 29 categories of hazard. It is the only hazard where the current level of occupancy should be considered before scoring. HHSRS states that a dwelling with one bedroom is suitable for up to two people regardless of age; two bedrooms for up to four people; three for up to six people; and four for up to seven people. Living rooms and kitchens are also considered.

Possession might also be obtained if the tenant has not paid the rent, or has broken some other term of the tenancy. The court has discretion, which is often used liberally, to decide whether to end the tenancy if the tenant can be shown to have caused a nuisance or annoyance to neighbours, has been convicted of immoral or illegal use of the premises, has damaged the property or allowed it to become damaged, or has damaged the furniture.

Likewise, if the landlord has arranged to sell or let the property because the tenant gave notice that he or she was giving up the tenancy, the tenant has assigned or sublet the whole of the property without the landlord's consent, the tenant was an employee of the landlord and the landlord requires the property for a new employee, the landlord needs the property for himself or herself or certain members of his or her family to live in and that greater hardship would not be caused by granting the order than by refusing to grant it (this does not normally apply if the tenant was a sitting tenant when the landlord bought the property), or the tenant has charged a subtenant more than the Rent Act permits.

Circumstances in which the court should grant the landlord possession include: when the landlord let his or her home with the intention of returning to live there again; the landlord let accommodation to which he or she intends to retire; the property was intended for farm workers or managers and has been let temporarily to an ordinary tenant; and where the landlord was a member of the regular armed forces at the time the letting was made and intended to live in the house at some future date.

To use these cases the landlord must have given prior written notice that he or she may apply for possession for this reason in the future. However, given the length of time that regulated tenancies will have been in existence (tenants will have been in situ for more than 20 years), cases where these grounds apply are now extremely rare.

The government booklet 'Regulated Tenancies' explains the rights and duties of landlords and tenants of regulated tenancies in more detail (**www.communities.gov.uk**).

What to Include in (Most) New Tenancy Agreements

The basics

As mentioned above, ASTs are the default form of tenancy agreement and when the new £100,000 rental limit comes into effect (see above) will be the more or less universal form of tenancy agreement for all new residential lets. The basic elements of the agreement are:

- the parties to the agreement and the date on which the agreement is made

- the start date and duration of the tenancy

- the amount and frequency of rental payments

- if the tenancy is for more than six months, the AST can include break clauses and also agreed rental increases at specified future dates

- responsibilities for general outgoings (rates, utility bills, repairs and maintenance) and other responsibilities of the two parties

- restrictions that landlords deem necessary – for example, a bar on redecoration without prior written consent from the landlord

- peculiarities to the property, such as a right of way over part of the garden, which need to be specified

- it is also good practice to include clauses dealing with late payment of rent and also with the termination of the tenancy

- when it comes to late payment of rent, landlords can specify a (reasonable) rate of interest that may be charged on overdue amounts and also make tenants responsible for any debt collection costs should these arise

- sometimes tenants leave possessions behind. A reasonable condition would be to say that the landlord may remove and store any possessions left by a tenant for (say) 28 days after which he or she may, after giving the tenant due notice, dispose of them – the tenant remaining liable for reasonable removal, storage and disposal costs

- it is also reasonable to say that the premises must not be left unoccupied for more than, say, 21 days (or the maximum specified in the relevant insurance policy). The tenancy agreement can specify that if the property is left empty for any longer period the landlord will have reasonable cause to believe the tenant has abandoned the property.

Other possible restrictions include specifying that a particular room or area may not be used and is to be kept locked, requiring that tenants or their guests do not smoke indoors, or do not keep pets in the house. However, any clauses of this nature should not be so restrictive as to be unreasonable.

Additional clauses

Apart from the basics of on Assured Shorthold Tenancy agreement listed above (covering such requirements as address, rent, details of the deposit, its purpose and protection, recital of statutory rights and responsibilities, and inclusion of prior notice of the statutory grounds for possession that may be used) there are other additional clauses that, if appropriate, it benefits the landlord to include. Below are some suggestions.

Included (re-phrased in suitable legal form) might be the requirements that the tenant or tenants shall:

- register for and pay the council tax

- put all utility supplies in his, her, or their own name or names and to pay all bills that result

- pay the television licence fee

- advise the landlord promptly of any defects and disrepair which are his or her duty to rectify

- keep the interior of the property clean and in good repair

- make good all damage and breakages to the property and landlord's contents caused by the tenant or tenants (with the exception of fair wear and tear and accidental damage by fire)

- regularly clean all the windows both inside and out

- keep the property warm and sufficiently aired and take all precautions reasonably necessary to prevent water leaks

- use reasonable endeavours to keep the property free from pests and vermin, and to advise the landlord promptly of any infestation of insects or vermin

- keep the garden in good order

- not make any internal or external alterations or additions to the property

- not tamper or interfere with appliances, wiring, plumbing or meters

- not carry out any redecoration without the prior written consent of the landlord

- not erect any television aerial, satellite dish, or radio mast, or install cable television, without the prior written consent of the landlord

- not engage any contractor or incur any expenditure on behalf of the landlord (except in case of emergency) without prior written approval

- not use or keep in the property any type of stove, heater, or lamp or other equipment whose presence or use might endanger the property or those within

- not install or change any locks or security codes without the landlord's prior written consent

- not leave the property unoccupied without locking and securing all windows and external doors and setting any security devices provided

- not leave the property unoccupied or vacant for any extended period of more than, say, 21 days without first giving written notice to the landlord of the intention to do so (it is also wise to include an abandonment clause to the effect that if it should come to the attention of the landlord that the property has not been occupied for more than 21 days, the tenant has not given the landlord notice of the absence, and landlord has reasonable cause to believe the tenant no longer lives there, then he or she may treat the let as having been abandoned. In such circumstances the landlord has the right to bring the agreement to an end and re-enter the property)

- not keep any pets without the previous written consent of the landlord

- use the property only for the purpose of a private residence and not use it for any profession, business, or trade, or for any illegal, immoral, or improper purpose

- not to obstruct any access to the premises

- not to keep, park, or store any boat, caravan, commercial or similar vehicle at or near the property

- not to do anything that may be or may become a nuisance or annoyance to neighbours

- not to do anything that may render the landlord's insurance cover invalid (a copy of the insurance policy to be provided to the tenant)

- not to bring into or store in the property any items of furniture that do not comply with the Furniture and Furnishings (Fire) (Safety) Regulations (**www.opsi.gov.uk**), nor any unsafe or untested appliances

- not to sublet any part of the property or take in a lodger

- not to assign the tenancy without the prior written consent of the landlord

- to forward without delay any correspondence addressed to the landlord and to inform him or her promptly of any notice affecting the property which may be served on the tenant

- subject to being given not less than 24 hours' prior notice, to allow the landlord and/or his or her agents or contractors to enter the property at reasonable times to inspect the property or to make necessary repairs, or to comply with a legal obligation

- subject to being giving not less than 24 hours' prior notice, to allow the landlord and/or his or her agents to enter the property at reasonable hours in the day to conduct viewings for prospective new tenants or buyers

- upon being giving notice in writing or necessary repairs or redecoration, or other work which is the responsibility of the tenant to complete, and the tenant having failed to complete this work within a reasonable time, to permit the landlord or his or her agent to enter the property to carry out such repairs (the reasonable cost of which shall be payable by the tenant)

- to pay to the landlord all reasonable costs and expenses of legal action necessarily taken by the landlord in connection with any breach of tenant obligations

- at the end of tenancy, to return items listed in the inventory (or their replacements) and not to remove any

- at the end of tenancy, leave the property free from rubbish and in a condition consistent with the performance of the tenant's obligations, and to remove all possessions (the landlord will store any possessions that are left for a reasonable time – say 28 days – and if the items are not collected within this time, may dispose of them at the tenant's expense

- at the end of tenancy, to return all keys and security devices or codes, and to pay all reasonable charges incurred by the landlord in securing the property against re-entry where the keys are not returned

- to pay interest at a specified rate above Bank base rate (also known as the Repro rate, this is rate set each month by the Bank of England's Monetary Policy Committee as the benchmark for other interest rates, including personal loans and mortgages), or any other published official rate of interest, on any rent or any other money payable by the tenants to the landlord that is outstanding longer than 14 days of the due date

- reimburse the landlord, at the end of the tenancy, reasonable professional cleaning costs for carpets, curtains, linens, bedding, upholstery and similar articles.

This list is not exhaustive, and when drawing up, amending or instructing their solicitors to draw up tenancy agreements, landlords should consider what other reasonable constraints and obligations they need to write into the contract.

Note that disabled tenants (those with "a physical or mental impairment which has a substantial and long-term adverse effect on his ability to carry out normal day-to-day activities") have a right under the Disability Discrimination Acts (2005 and 1995: copies can be downloaded from www.opsi.gov.uk) to request reasonable changes to their tenancy agreements that would put them on an equal footing with other tenants. So they might request, for example, the lifting of an exclusion of pets to accommodate a guide dog. The landlord might be found to have discriminated against the disabled tenant if he or she refused such a change without reasonable cause.

Multiple signatories and tenancies

Tenancy agreements may be in the name of one tenant or of a number – for example, a couple living together as partners. From the landlord's point of view, two or more signatories to the AST are better than one since each will be *jointly* and *severally* liable for the full rent – meaning that if one does not or cannot pay, the other tenant is responsible in law for the entire amount.

Houses can also be divided into multiple tenancies where each tenant has exclusive use of a particular part of the property (say a bedroom) specified in the tenancy agreement, with access to and use of common areas. It makes sense to have multiple rather than joint tenancies where the tenants are not related and may intend to live in the property for different periods.

This makes no difference to the HMO (house in multiple occupation) status of the property since this now depends on the number of people living in the property and their relationship to each other rather than on whether they have separate or joint tenancy agreements.

Student lets are likely to be HMOs – and if so, and of three stories or more, a licence will be required (see Chapters 4 and 5 above). A licence may be required in any case, depending on local requirements. Whether an HMO or not, and whether let as a joint or a number of separate tenancies, student tenancy agreements usually contain special clauses that recognise the special circumstances of students (they will want to secure a home well in advance of the start of the academic term, probably when existing tenants are still in place, but to live in the property only during term time).

To help overcome potential loss that would occur if students do not leave on agreed dates, landlords often include a stipulation that additional costs that would result are to be borne by the students who refuse to leave. Also, it is usual to charge rent at different rates – a term-time rate, when students are in residence, and a *holding rate* to cover out of term periods when the students will not be resident.

Ending Agreements

Tenancy agreements will be for a fixed term – ASTs are, as noted above, usually for six months – and expire at the end of that term. However, tenancies remain in place until the landlord or the tenant or tenants give notice. Landlords need to be particularly cautious when seeking possession of their property – simply entering a property and forcing tenants to leave is a criminal offence, even if proper notice has been given.

Tenancies are ended by notice being given and the tenants leaving. If they do not leave when required to do so, landlords must obtain a court order to make them quit the property.

Most tenancies do not come to this and tenants leave in an orderly way.

Even so, all legal niceties should be observed. Care should be taken in completing ASTs in the first place, and in particular in the spelling of names and in setting out correct postal addresses in full. They should be duly signed and dated (two copies – one for the landlord and one for the tenant) and kept safe. If the agreement is signed before the date the tenant obtains possession, signatures should be witnessed by an independent and unrelated person.

This is covered in more detail in the later chapter dealing with *Possession*.

For further information about different types of tenancies, see the government booklet 'Assured and Assured Shorthold Tenancies: A guide for landlords' – **www.communities.gov.uk**.

Judges must consider 'reasonableness' from all angles

In 2009, Rent Act-protected tenant Patricia Whitehouse was successful in preventing her landlord moving her to alternative accommodation in order that the landlord could sell the Hampstead flat she and her husband had lived in for 46 years. But she had to go to the Court of Appeal to win her case.

There, Lord Justice Rimer said the London County Court had been wrong in originally finding in favour of Mrs Whitehouse's landlord, Dr Loi Lee.

The reason was not that the accommodation Dr Lee proposed to provide her tenant was not suitable – although neither Mrs Whitehouse or her husband, who had recently died, had liked the flat that had been bought a mile up the road, and had worried that associated service charges would cause extra expense, they did not appeal against the County Court decision that it was suitable. Dr Loi Lee, who owned the flat along with adjacent properties with her brother and sister, had even offered to contribute towards moving costs and service charges.

The reason that the appeal succeeded was that the judge hearing the County Court case had not considered the effect on both tenants and landlord, both if possession was granted, and if it were not granted. The law, established by legal precedent, required that the test of reasonableness take all these factors into account.

In this case there was no doubt that Mr and Mrs Whitehouse would be adversely affected – Mrs Whitehouse was a "valuable, popular and respected member of a local community", said Lord Justice Rimer. However, this was not the issue. The critical question, which the County Court judge did not address, was the effect on the owners of the property if no order were made.

It was reasonable for them to want to sell the property for its maximum value but they had advanced no case of hardship if they could not so sell. Also, refusal of an order would not mean that they would lose the opportunity of realising the full value of Mrs Whitehouse's flat forever. And since the owners did not need to sell with vacant possession, they could, if they chose, sell subject to the tenants' occupation, albeit realising a smaller return.

Delaying the owners their opportunity to sell the property with vacant possession was to do no more than that – delaying the opportunity. After all, they had bought the property in 1969, when Mr and Mrs Whitehouse were already living there, and they could not have been certain that they would ever be entitled to evict the tenants.

The two other Appeal Court Judges, Lord Justice Aikens and Lord Justice Waller, agreed with the ruling.

8.

Rent, Rent Controls, Rent Increases and Rent Arrears

Rent Controls

In general there have been few rent controls on private rented property since 1989. However, some remnants of the previous regime of controls remain. These primarily concern *regulated tenancies* – in the main, private rented tenancies that were begun before 15 January 1989 when the law changed. But there are also some other controls which have been exercised through Rent Officers employed by local authorities, the Rent Service (since April 2009 most functions have been undertaken by the Valuation Office Agency — **www.voa.gov.uk**) and the Residential Property Tribunal Service (**www.rpts.gov.uk**).

Regulated tenancies

Regulated tenancies give tenants considerable security of tenure (a landlord needs to obtain a court order to end the tenancy) and also the comfort that in most circumstances their rents cannot be increased more frequently than every other year, and then only by a limited amount.

Either landlord or tenants of regulated tenancies may apply to the local rent service to have a *fair rent* registered. Fair rents are those set by the Rent Service under the rules set out in the Rent Act 1977.

All fair rents are recorded in the local rent register. The Rent Service must consider:

- all the circumstances except the personal circumstances of the landlord and the tenant

- the state of repair of the house or flat, its character

- its locality and age, plus the quantity and state of furniture that is provided

- any premium lawfully paid.

It may not consider:

- any disrepair for which the tenant is responsible

- any improvements that the tenant has made which he or she did not need to under the terms of his or her tenancy.

The Rent Service adjust for premiums due to a shortage of similar houses or flats available for letting in the area.

Once registered, the fair rent cannot be changed unless:

- the landlord and tenant apply jointly

- there has been a change of circumstances (for example, major repairs, improvements or a change in the terms of the tenancy) or

- the landlord applies one year and nine months after the effective date of the existing registration. But in this case the new registration will still not take effect until two years from the effective date of the existing registration.

Unless there is a change in circumstances, a *fair rent* may only be increased to the current *maximum fair rent* – arrived at by a calculation linked to the official inflation rate plus an additional amount. This provision introduced in recognition that in 1989 the *fair rent* of regulated tenancies would have been considerably lower than an open market rent.

The maximum fair rent is calculated as:

- the existing registered rent, plus

- the percentage change in inflation measured by the Retail Prices Index (all items) since the rent was last registered, plus

- an additional 7.5% for the first time the rent was re-registered after January 1999 or an additional 5% for all subsequent registrations.

Disputes about the amount of fair rent are referred to the appropriate rent assessment panel – independent tribunals of two or three people operated through the Residential Property Tribunal Service (see below).

The RPTS

The Residential Property Tribunal Service (**www.rpts.gov.uk**) is the umbrella organisation for the five regional rent assessment panels providing an independent tribunal service in England for settling disputes involving private rented and leasehold property. It can deal with rent disputes concerning controlled tenancies and assured tenancies and Housing Act appeals and applications, such as applications for and appeals against Empty Dwelling Management Orders (orders which local authorities can seek which allow them to take over the running of residential property that has been left empty for more than six months – these are dealt with in more detail in Chapter 11, 'Local Housing Authorities').

The five rent assessment panels covering England are:

London
10 Alfred Place
London
WC1E 7LR
telephone 020 7446 7700

Covering all London boroughs.

Eastern
Great Eastern House
Tenison Road
Cambridge
CB1 2TR
telephone 0845 100 2616

Covering Bedfordshire, Berkshire, Buckinghamshire, Cambridgeshire, Hertfordshire, Oxfordshire, Suffolk, Norfolk, Northamptonshire, Luton, Milton Keynes, Peterborough, Southend-on-Sea, Thurrock and Essex.

Midland
2nd Floor East Wing
Ladywood House
45-46 Stephenson Street
Birmingham
B2 4DH
telephone 0845 100 2615

Covering Staffordshire, Shropshire, Herefordshire, Worcestershire, West Midlands, Warwickshire, Leicestershire, Derbyshire, Nottinghamshire, Rutland, Stoke-on-Trent and The Wrekin.

Northern
20th Floor
Sunley Tower Piccadilly Plaza
Manchester
M1 4BF
telephone 0845 100 2614

Covering Blackburn, Blackpool, Cheshire, Cumbria, Darlington, Durham, East Riding of Yorkshire, Greater Manchester, Halton, Hartlepool, Kingston-upon-Hull, Lancashire, Lincolnshire, Merseyside, Middlesborough, North East Lincolnshire, North Lincolnshire, North Yorkshire, Northumberland, Redcar & Cleveland, South Yorkshire, Stockton-on-Tees, Tyne & Wear, Warrington, West Yorkshire and York.

Southern
1st Floor
1 Market Avenue
Chichester
West Sussex
PO19 1JU
telephone 0845 100 2617

Covering Hampshire, East and West Sussex, Surrey, Kent, Isle of Wight, The Medway Towns, Portsmouth, Southampton, Brighton and Hove, Wiltshire, Dorset, Devon, The County of Bath and North East Somerset, North West Somerset, Somerset, Bournemouth, City of Bristol, Cornwall and Isle of Scilly, Gloucester, South Gloucester, Plymouth, Poole, Swindon and Torbay.

> **The rent assessment panel for Wales**
> 1st Floor
> West Wing
> Southgate House
> Wood Street
> Cardiff
> CF10 1EW
> telephone 029 2023 1687

The government booklet *Regulated Tenancies* can be downloaded from **www.communities.gov.uk**.

The Rent Acts (Maximum Fair Rent) Order 1999 (**www.opsi.gov.uk**) limits the amount of rent that can be charged by linking increases to the Retail Prices Index. Further information is available in the Information leaflets listed below.

An application form for registration of a fair rent can be downloaded from the Valuation Office Agency (**www.voa.gov.uk**).

In general there are no appeals possible against the decision of a rent assessment panel, except to the High Court on a point of law.

Assured tenancies

Assured (as opposed to assured shorthold) tenancies can continue for some time. If allowed to become assured periodic tenancies, the term of the periodic tenancy will usually be the same as the original fixed-term tenancy – so if for one year, then for one year more.

However, if the need arises landlords may seek a change in rent and other terms during an assured periodic tenancy. Section 6(2) of the Housing Act 1988 allows either the landlord or his or her tenant or tenants to apply, within set time limits, for variation in the terms of the agreement with or without a consequential change in the rent.

If, for example, the landlord wants to increase the rent and gives notice to this effect but the tenant disagrees, the tenant can apply to the relevant Residential Property Tribunal Service to have a rent assessment panel set the terms of the tenancy.

Who Pays for What?

There are always outgoings associated with property, and also letting costs to be met such as agents' fees and advertising costs. Some of these costs will be met by landlords (with suitable adjustment factored into the rent) and some by tenants. There can sometimes be uncertainty about who pays for what. There shouldn't be. Such matters should be explained and agreed at the outset and written into tenancy agreements.

For example, it is good practice for tenancy agreements to specify that tenants are responsible for registering and paying council tax and for making sure all bills for utilities, including gas, electricity, water and telephone, and for television licences, are made out to them and are paid by them.

In general landlords will be responsible for paying for:

- an energy performance certificate

- annual gas safety certificates

- council tax, where the property is an HMO or the landlord is also resident in the property (this will be apportioned and charged back to the tenants by the landlord, although full-time students resident in an HMO should be entitled to council tax exemption)

- council tax when the property is not let (council tax applies to the property as a whole and is apportioned on a daily basis)

- service charges, if applicable

- ground rent, if applicable

- letting agent fees

- repairs and maintenance to the structure of the property and contents supplied

- insurance of property and landlord's contents

- maintenance contracts for boilers and the like

- deposit protection fees

- agents' commission.

Tenants will be responsible for paying for:

- council tax

- all utilities supplied to the property

- television licences

- insurance of tenant's contents

- damage or loss caused to landlord supplied contents, other than normal wear and tear.

Agents and landlords sometimes require tenants to pay for credit checks and other costs when setting up a tenancy and for cleaning at the expiry of a tenancy.

Rent Arrears

Rent arrears, accumulated when tenants fall behind with their monthly rent can be a bane for any landlord. It is important to do the utmost to avoid arrears building up.

This starts at the outset with proper credit checks, sight of the tenant's or tenants' bank accounts, and details of his, her or their employment. But even *good credit risks* can sometimes move into arrears. While landlords will wish to sympathise with the plight of good

❝ If tenants fall into arrears and are not prepared to talk about the problem, landlords have no alternative but to press ahead with collection proceedings. **❞**

tenants whose circumstances have changed, action should be taken to make tenants aware that arrears are not acceptable and if necessary to come to some agreement for dealing with these. For example, landlords can offer to allow tenants to spread the making good of arrears over a few months on condition they provide a guarantor (assuming there is not one already in place).

Collection proceedings

If tenants fall into arrears and are not prepared to talk about the problem, landlords have no alternative but to press ahead with collection proceedings. These should start with a series of (perhaps) three letters, sent a few days apart, each reminding the tenant in more forceful terms that the rent is overdue and what the consequences might be.

Landlords have a number of means of pressing their claims. The first is the threat, and if necessary pursuit, of possession proceedings leading to eviction. Application will have to be made to the court on what is known as 'ground 8' – one of the grounds for possession specified in the Housing Act 1988 (see Chapter 10). This applies if the tenant owes at least two months' rent (if the tenancy is on a monthly basis) or eight weeks' rent (if it is on a weekly basis), both at the point the landlord gave notice seeking possession and at the date of the court hearing. If proved, this is a *mandatory ground*, meaning the court is obliged to grant possession to the landlord.

As tenancy agreements normally specify that rent is to be paid one month in advance, tenants are likely to be two months in arrears as soon as they miss two payments in a row.

Application can also be made at the same time for possession on 'ground 10' – that the tenant was behind with his or her rent both when the landlord served notice seeking possession and when he or she began court proceedings, and 'ground 11' – that even if the tenant was not behind with his or her rent when the landlord started possession proceedings, the tenant has been persistently late in paying the rent. These are *discretionary* grounds, meaning courts have the power to decide whether or not to grant possession.

The process can be started online by going to:
www.hmcourts-service.gov.uk

Small Claims Court

Whether or not possession is sought or granted, landlords can use the small claims court to recover unpaid rent as well as any other monies owned by tenants. This is a relatively simple procedure and can be commenced online by going to **www.moneyclaim.gov.uk**. However, a current address will be needed to serve the claim, so if the tenant has moved out some groundwork might be necessary. This is where the importance of records comes in, since landlords should have asked for the address of a next of kin when the tenant first applied.

There will be court costs (landlords can include these in their claim and also add interest). However, other legal costs cannot be reclaimed in Small Claims Court proceedings.

If the landlord is successful in court but the tenant still refuses to pay, one option open in the case of employed tenants is to seek an attachment of earnings – a relatively simple process in which the employer is instructed by the Court to make weekly or monthly deductions from pay: these amounts are paid to the court and subsequently to the landlord. For more on this, go to **www.hmcourts-service.gov.uk**.

Fair rent assessment in practice

In 2007 the London Rent Assessment Panel approved a fair rent of £728 per month for a Camberwell property whose open market rent it acknowledged to be £1,800.

A fair rent of £648.50 per month had been registered in 2005. In 2007 the landlord proposed that this be nearly doubled to £1,200 per month. However, the Rent Officer decided the fair rent should be £728.50. The tenant thought this still too much and appealed to the Rent Assessment Committee.

The house, which was probably built over 100 years ago, was of four floors, including a basement and was situated "in a pleasant residential area", according to the rent assessment panel. There was no off-street parking.

When the committee inspected the property it found it to be in good condition internally and externally.

The tenant told the panel that she had carried out all internal and external repairs and decoration for many years and had not asked the landlord to do so.

She had also made improvements at her own expense, including upgrading the electrics, installing a new kitchen, and adding a bath and water heaters.

The committee said it reached its decision as to a fair rent taking into account the age, location and state of repair of the property. It also disregarded the effect of the tenant's improvements and any disrepair or defects attributable to the tenant on the rental value of the property.

It also followed the precedent set by two Court of Appeal cases in which the court emphasised that ordinarily a fair rent would be the market rent as signified by assured tenancy rents being paid for comparable properties but discounted for any part of those rents that could be attributed to *scarcity* – in other words, a similar rent to that which would be paid by private rented sector tenants if there were sufficient rental properties available to meet demand (seemingly something of an impossible task).

The committee decided that a market rent for the property would have been £1,800 per month. However, it said this particular property, as provided by the landlord, was "not in the condition considered usual for a modern letting at a market rent".

This meant it would adjust the hypothetical rent of £1,800 per month to allow for this, deducting £40 per week because there was no central heating, £15 for white goods, £25 for carpets and curtains, and £25 for the tenant's liability for internal decoration and repair. On top of this, the committee made a deduction of £95 per week to allow for the improvements made by the tenant.

In total the deductions came to £870 per month, making the net market rent £930 per month. This would have been the fair rent but for the provisions of Rent Acts (Maximum Fair Rent) Order 1999 which limits increases to an additional 7.5% for the first time a rent is re-registered after January 1999 and to an additional 5% for all subsequent registrations. This meant the maximum fair rent that could be registered was £728 per month.

9.

Repairs and Property Contents

Repairs

Except in the case of fixed-term tenancies of more than seven years, landlords are responsible under the Landlord and Tenant Act 1985 for repairs to:

- the structure and exterior of the dwelling
- basins, sinks, baths and other sanitary installations in the dwelling, and
- heating and hot water installations.

However, landlords are not generally responsible for repairs arising from damage caused by their tenants, or for rebuilding the property in the case of damage by fire, flood or other unavoidable accident. Nor do they have to repair anything which the tenant has a right to take away unless, in some circumstances, the damage was caused as a result of the landlord's failure to carry out his or her repairing obligations.

Under common law, a tenant must use rental property in a responsible way. They must take proper care of it. For example, they should turn off the water if there is a risk of burst pipes when going away, and unblock sinks when clogged up by waste. They should not damage the property and should make sure that their family and guests do not do so. If they do, they may be responsible for the damage.

Under the Rent Act 1977, the Housing Act 1985 and the Housing Act 1988, landlords are entitled to seek possession when tenants or someone living with them damage the rental property (ground 13, "the condition of the property has got worse because of the behaviour of the tenant or any other person living there", and ground 15, "the condition of the furniture in the property has got worse because it has been ill treated by the tenant or any other person living there").

Tenancy agreements will usually set out the rights and liabilities of the parties and may cover the procedure for getting repairs undertaken. Should landlords who have been told about the necessity for repairs by their tenants fail to have these made, tenants can:

- bring proceedings against their landlord – if successful they may be awarded damages as well as obtaining an order for repairs to be undertaken

- contact their local council – which has powers, under the Housing Act 2004, to carry out an assessment of the property using the Housing Health and Safety Rating System (HHSRS).

Tenants sometimes claim a right to have the repairs made and to deduct the amount from rent. The legal position here is difficult and in theory could give rise to a justification for possession proceedings, although in practical terms landlords may have difficulty recovering amounts deducted in this way.

There is an implied term in tenancy agreements under the Rent Act 1977 and the Housing Act 1988 that tenants will allow their landlords access to the property to carry out repairs they are entitled to undertake. Where landlords are responsible for repairs, they, or their agent, may enter the premises at reasonable times of the day to inspect its condition and state of repair, but may do so only after giving tenants at least 24 hours' notice in writing.

If a regulated tenant will not give his or her consent for work to be carried out for which the landlord has a local authority grant, then the landlord may apply to the court for an order to enter and carry out the works. An order can be made subject to conditions about the time at which the work is carried out and about alternative accommodation arrangements.

For more details, see the government booklet 'Repairs' at **www.communities.gov.uk**.

Dancing on the tables

Maintenance and repairs can cause problems between landlords and tenants – especially when one or both are unsure of their own responsibilities – or unwilling to fulfil them adequately.

Tenants have been known to ask landlords to replace light bulbs or kill ants, or, more reasonably, to do something about unpleasant smells or rustling under the floorboards.

Some tenants are less careful with the property they rent than others.

In 2009 Carolyn Lorimer was shocked to find pictures of a rowdy party in her rented Folkestone flat posted on the website Facebook. Besides dancing on her tables, the mayhem which the tenants had apparently been happy to reveal to the world included a broken television and ripped wallpaper. And she soon spotted other pictures that had been posted and which showed yet more damage done to her two-bedroom property during the eight months she had let it to a "respectable couple" (the agency's phrase). These included burns to the carpets and holes in the wall.

She immediately started possession proceedings but the tenants did not wait to be forced to move. Already behind with their rent, they fled, leaving a mountain of unpaid utility bills.

Identifying such unruly tenants in advance is not always easy, which only goes to underline the need for thorough pre-letting checks, including referencing, and for regular inspection visits during tenancies.

* * *

Landlords, of course, cannot simply up and leave, and their failures are likely to catch up with them, as High Wycombe landlord Itlaf Hussain found out.

In 2010 his local council took him to court largely over the state of repair of his HMO property.

Wycombe District Council environmental health officers visited his property numerous times over a period of months and each time they found fault. On one occasion they concluded that emergency electrical work was needed to make the property safe.

Hussain pleaded guilty to the charges against him and was fined a total of £6,758 and ordered to pay costs of £1,743 and a victim surcharge of £15.

For failing to display his name, address and telephone number in a prominent position in the rented property, he was fined £500, and for failing to display notices clearly showing tenants the means of escape from fire, another £1,000. He was also fined £1,000 for failing to ensure the drainage system was maintained in a good clean and working condition (inspectors found that the soil pipe of the toilet had a hole in it, was not properly connected to the drainage system and was leaking), and £1,000 also for failing to maintain common parts of the property in a safe and working condition (inspectors found 24 electrical defects including a 13-amp power point in the shower cubicle, no electrical earth for the property and bare live wires protruding from an outside wall).

Failure to ensure the garden was kept in a safe and tidy condition (officers found the garden shed was propped up and in danger of collapse and floorboards with rusty nails protruding were stored in the garden) brought another £500 fine. And finally Hussain was fined another £1,000 for failing to maintain the gas cooker in good repair – neither could he provide a Gas Safe certificate for the property.

Councillor Chris Watson, Cabinet Member for Homes and Housing at Wycombe District Council said: "Our officers work with local landlords to ensure that they are aware of their obligations to tenants. In most cases, responsible landlords work with us to ensure that the properties they rent out are safe. Regrettably, in some instances, landlords take no remedial action and tenants' lives may even be put at risk as a result. In these cases, we can and do prosecute."

Property Contents

Whether or not property is offered for rent as furnished or unfurnished will largely depend upon local demand. If potential tenants are only interested in furnished property, it is no good trying to buck the trend, and vice versa.

Whether the property is offered furnished or unfurnished will have no effect on fundamental landlord and tenant rights, though, as we shall see, furnished properties entail a duty of care on the part of landlords towards their tenants which means that they must ensure that all appliances are safe and in good working order, and that all furnishings meet fire safety standards. Whether or not the property is let furnished, landlords still have a duty to provide adequate ventilation, space heating and water heating.

Defining furnished

There is no legal definition of what constitutes *furnished* or *unfurnished* rental property. It is sometimes suggested that furnished property should contain sufficient appliances, furniture and utensils to allow a tenant to live there without having to add anything.

However, what is certain is that what is provided at the outset and included in the inventory (explained later in the chapter) signed by tenant and landlord, should be there throughout the tenancy and maintained in good working order. This may mean that on occasion landlords have to replace appliances or even broken and worn out furniture during the course of a tenancy.

This, of course, does not give tenants the right to do other than treat contents with reasonable care. They can be asked to pay for damage, other than normal wear and tear, and losses.

Furniture and appliances

Gas appliances, including boilers, flues, gas fires and cookers should be checked annually so that there is a current gas safety certificate (certificates cover a 12-month period). Furniture and furnishings must comply with the Furniture and Furnishings (Fire) (Safety) Regulations (**www.opsi.gov.uk**).

The regulations cover:

- beds: bed bases, headboards, mattresses, pillows

- sofa beds and futons, and upholstered garden furniture

- settees, armchairs, dining chairs, upholstered stools

- cushions, including seat pads, floor cushions and beanbags

- baby equipment and nursery furniture, including cots and mattresses, playpens, highchairs, prams.

Furniture made before 1950, bed clothes, loose covers for mattresses, pillowcases, curtains, carpets, and sleeping bags are excluded. The regulations do not cover tenant's own furniture, although prudent landlords will include a clause in the tenancy agreement prohibiting tenants from bringing in non-complying items of furniture (and unsafe or untested appliances).

The regulations require that rental accommodation let since 1 January 1997 must contain only furniture and furnishings that meet fire resistance standards as evidenced by a fire resistance label – look for labels headed 'Carelessness Causes Fire'.

If there should be a fire and it is found that furnishings and furniture were not compliant with the regulations, landlords are likely to find themselves charged with supply of non-compliant furniture, fillings or fabrics in the course of business. If found guilty, the maximum penalty is six months' imprisonment or a fine of £5,000 – or both.

The regulations place the onus on the landlord to prove he or she has taken *all reasonable steps* to ensure the furniture supplied to the tenant or tenants is in compliance with their requirements.

If in any doubt about the suitability of furniture and furnishings, landlords should consult their local Trading Standards office, which will have responsibility for enforcing the regulations (the address and telephone number of your local Trading Standards office can be obtained from the Trading Standards Institute website at **www.tradingstandards.gov.uk**). Receipts for new furniture should be retained as proof of purchase from reputable retailers.

Essential items, to be returned in same condition

Besides basic furniture, furnished accommodation will also come with kitchen utensils, cutlery, crockery and other items including carpets and other flooring, light fittings, pictures, mirrors and ornaments. Naturally landlords require that these items be returned at the end of a tenancy in the same condition (subject to fair wear and tear) in which they have been supplied. Deposits, if taken, will – in part at least – be to cover the cost of breakages and replacements.

❝ The landlord should be in a position to provide full evidence of damage or losses in the form of an inventory signed by the tenant. ❞

To be sure that all is returned as expected (and to provide proof of what has been provided should this not be the case), all those items provided – including furniture and furnishings, appliances and utensils, light fitting and ornaments, cutlery and crockery, and garden tools and equipment – need to be listed at the outset and a receipt for their supply provided by the tenant or tenants.

Such inventories should be in sufficient detail to identify each item and its condition when supplied. Some landlords supplement written, room-by-room inventories with photographic evidence (pictures or sometimes videos). Others rely on the services of their agents or a professional inventory company to ensure they have adequate records of what has been supplied by way of contents.

Tenants should be given time to check that inventories are correct (two copies should be provided) and asked to sign the landlords' copy (and copies of any pictures or any video disks).

This documentation should be retained during the tenancy and at least until return or otherwise of the deposit (if any) has been resolved. Should there be a dispute over the deposit this will be handled according to the rules of the deposit-protection scheme used and the landlord should be in a position to provide full evidence of damage or losses in the form of an inventory signed by the tenant.

Insurance

Notwithstanding, it is the landlord's responsibility to insure contents provided to tenants – although tenants should be reminded that it is their own duty to insure their own property, including any appliances or furniture they have introduced into the rented property. (For more on insurance see chapter 14 'Insurance'.)

Abandoned (or stored) contents

Tenants' contents can sometimes cause a problem if they are not removed at the end of a tenancy, or if, for example, a tenancy is simply abandoned. To make sure they have a legal right to deal with such contents – by storing for a specified period and then, if they are still not collected, disposing of them – landlords should make sure their tenancy agreements include a clause to this effect.

Likewise landlords sometimes leave their own personal possessions stored in rental properties. In such circumstances this should be made clear at the outset and if a substantial amount of space is required – such as a room or garage – this should be written into the tenancy agreement so that tenants cannot later argue that they did not have access to all of the space for which they were paying rent. In general landlords should never leave personal documents in rented properties as even if stored in an *off limits* part of the property, there is always the chance that a dishonest tenant could gain access to them and use the information, such as that contained in birth certificates, driving licences, utility bills, even personal correspondence, to commit identity fraud.

Sweet smell of unwanted contents

Landlords sometimes find tenants bring unwelcome items into their rented homes – sometimes very unwelcome.

In recent years there has been a spate of incidences in which rented homes have been used as cannabis factories, with numerous plants filling up unwitting landlords' houses.

The pattern is often the same. A tenant turns up and rents a property for six months or a year, paying by cash in advance for the whole period.

After the tenant moves in, the curtains are rarely if ever opened and the door is never answered. The landlord finds it impossible to contact the tenant.

Meanwhile the tenant has probably illegally tampered with the electric meter or mains cable to power the bright lights and fans needed to grow the plants. Holes may have been punched in the walls to aid ventilation, floorboards lifted to get at wiring and pipes, and furniture moved out or trashed to accommodate plants, equipment and fertiliser.

Eventually somebody notices an unusual (to some, familiar) smell coming from the property. The police are called and break in. They find rooms full of plants but no tenants – nobody knows for sure who they are and they never reappear.

£50,000 in the master bedroom

Something of this kind has occurred in places such as as Walton in Surrey, Wokingham, Milton Keynes, Sheppey, Epsom, Kidderminster, Ewell, Redditch, Wolverhampton, and many more.

In Epsom 250 cannabis plants with a street value of £50,000 were found in a rented house after the landlord contacted the police. Officers had to wait to enter the property while electrical equipment and dangerous wiring was made safe. When they did go inside they found five rooms given over to cannabis plants.

A Wokingham landlord estimated £10,000 worth of damage had been done to his property to accommodate the growing of cannabis plants. The first he knew of this was when police contacted him following a raid on the house. They had been tipped off by a local resident.

In Burnley a cannabis factory was discovered after burglars broke into a rented property. Alerted by neighbours, police arrived and discovered over 500 cannabis plants. All but one room in the six-bedroom house had been converted to cannabis production, with high powered lamps and fans going at full tilt.

Landlord Ikram Haq said he was horrified to discover he been duped by his tenants in this way.

Cheshire police say cannabis farms have been discovered in large towns such as Warrington, Macclesfield and Northwich, but also in rural areas like Tarvin.

"You may not realise it but the farms themselves pose a serious threat to your health. They require the large quantities of fertilizers and pesticides being stored and are often connected illegally to the electricity supply, posing huge fire risks."

Signs to look for were said to be:

- a pungent and sweet smell on the street with no obvious source

- unusual levels of heat coming from a property and/or no frost or snow on the property when every house around is covered

- unusual noises at odd times, such as fans going constantly, or large items like sacks or drums being dragged around

- windows that are blacked out by heavy curtains or bin bags from the inside

- occupants who are rarely seen or seen at odd times

- the property seems unlived in or the residents are active at odd times of the day

- bulky items being taken into the property, such as barrels and drums

- the creation of new air vents or the use of industrial air vents in a domestic property.

10.

Possession

A ssured shorthold tenancy agreements *assure* landlords that they can regain possession of their properties at the end of those agreements, or, if they have been allowed to run on as *periodic tenancies*, during the periodic tenancy.

This does not mean landlords can take matters into their own hands and make tenants leave by force. Far from it. The Protection from Eviction Act 1977 makes it an offence, punishable by up to two years in jail, and/or a fine, for a landlord to:

- commit acts likely to interfere with the peace or comfort of a tenant or anyone living with them

- persistently withdraw or withhold services for which the tenant has a reasonable need to live in the premises as a home

- make a tenant leave their home, or stop using part of it

- do anything that stops a tenant doing the things they could normally expect to do

- take someone's home away from him or her unlawfully.

To gain possession landlords must follow some well-defined steps, issuing possession claims in the courts.

Approximately 22,000 did so in the last quarter of 2009, the Ministry of Justice reported in early 2010. Around 4,000 of the claims used the accelerated procedure (leading to 2,900 orders), while 28,000 used the standard County Court procedure (leading to 19,200 orders being made. Just under half of the orders made (49%) were suspended.

The First Step

The starting point for gaining possession legally, either when or after a fixed-term tenancy has run its course, is for the landlord to issue the tenant with what is usually referred to as a 'section 21' (referring to section 21 of the Housing Act 1988) notice to quit.

This notice must be in writing and allow at least two calendar months from the date the tenant receives the notice before possession is required. If the tenancy is fixed term, the notice may not require the tenant to quit the property less than six months after moving in, or, if the tenancy agreement specifies a longer fixed-term period, before the end of that period or before the date of any break clause in the tenancy agreement (as long as this is after at least six months). Notices may not be issued before tenancies commence.

There is no particular form of wording required. However, The Notices to Quit etc. (Prescribed Information) Regulations 1988 (**www.opsi.gov.uk**) require inclusion of a statement that:

1. *If the tenant or licensee does not leave the dwelling, the landlord or licensor must obtain an order for possession from the [County] court before the tenant or licensee can lawfully be evicted. The landlord or licensor cannot apply for such an order before the notice to quit or notice to determine has run out.*

2. *A tenant or licensee who does not know if he or she has any right to remain in possession after a notice to quit or a notice to determine runs out can obtain advice from a solicitor. Help with all or part of the cost of legal advice and assistance may be available under the Legal Aid Scheme. He or she should also be able to obtain information from a Citizens' Advice Bureau, a Housing Aid Centre or a rent service.*

Notices can be delivered in person or by post. Landlords should retain copies and any proof of delivery, such as special delivery slips.

If the Tenant Remains

Should a tenant, having received proper notice, not give up possession by the specified date, the landlord will be obliged to issue possession proceedings in the County Court using form 'N5: Claim form for possession of property'. This can be obtained online from the Court Service website: **www.hmcourts-service.gov.uk**. Provided the notice has been issued correctly, the Housing Act requires the court to grant possession.

Should the tenant still not move out, the landlord can apply for a warrant of execution (meaning an order that the court order be enforced – not a licence to kill troublesome tenants!) using form 'N325: Request for warrant for possession of land' (also obtainable from the Court Service website). This would allow bailiffs to be appointed who will oblige the tenant to leave.

Other Circumstances of Possession

Landlords can also seek to regain possession of their property during the course of assured and assured shorthold tenancies if particular circumstances arise – including, for example, rent falling into arrears. The reasons are listed in the 1988 Housing Act as various grounds for possession.

Grounds for possession

Assured and Assured Shorthold Tenancies

During the fixed term of an assured or shorthold tenancy, the landlord can only seek possession if one of grounds 2, 8, 10 to 15 or 17 apply and the terms of the tenancy make provision for it to be ended on any of these grounds. When the fixed term of an assured tenancy ends, possession can be sought on any of the grounds. When the fixed term of a shorthold tenancy ends, the landlord does not have to give any grounds for possession.

Mandatory grounds on which the court must order possession

(A prior notice ground means that the landlord must have notified the tenant in writing before the tenancy started that he or she might seek possession on this ground.)

Ground 1: a prior notice ground

The property was previously the landlord's only or main home. Or, so long as the landlord or someone before him or her did not buy the property after the tenancy started, the landlord (or landlord's spouse) requires it to live in as his or her main home.

Ground 2: a prior notice ground

The property is subject to a mortgage which was granted before the tenancy started and the lender, usually a bank or building society, wants to sell it, normally to pay off mortgage arrears.

Ground 3: a prior notice ground

The tenancy is for a fixed term of not more than 8 months and at some time during the 12 months before the tenancy started, the property was let for a holiday.

Ground 4: a prior notice ground

The tenancy is for a fixed term of not more than 12 months and at some time during the 12 months before the tenancy started, the property was let to students by an educational establishment such as a university or college.

Ground 5: a prior notice ground

The property is held for use for a minister of religion and is now needed for that purpose.

Ground 6

The landlord intends to substantially redevelop the property and cannot do so with the tenant there. This ground cannot be used where the landlord, or someone before him or her, bought the property with an existing tenant, or where the work could be carried out without the tenant having to move. The tenant's reasonable removal expenses, as assessed by the court, will have to be paid by the landlord.

Ground 7

The former tenant, who must have had a contractual periodic tenancy or statutory periodic tenancy, has died in the 12 months before possession proceedings started and there is no one living there who has a right to succeed to the tenancy.

Ground 8

The tenant owed at least two months' rent if the tenancy is on a monthly basis or 8 weeks' rent if it is on a weekly basis, both when the landlord gave notice seeking possession and at the date of the court hearing.

Discretionary grounds on which the court may order possession

Ground 9

Suitable alternative accommodation is available for the tenant, or will be when the court order takes effect. The tenant's removal expenses will have to be paid.

Ground 10

The tenant was behind with his or her rent both when the landlord served notice seeking possession and when he or she began court proceedings.

Ground 11

Even if the tenant was not behind with his or her rent when the landlord started possession proceedings, the tenant has been persistently late in paying the rent.

Ground 12

The tenant has broken one or more of the terms of the tenancy agreement, except the obligation to pay rent.

Ground 13

The condition of the property has got worse because of the behaviour of the tenant or any other person living there.

Ground 14

The tenant, or someone living in or visiting the property:

(a) has caused, or is likely to cause, a nuisance or annoyance to someone living in or visiting the locality; or

(b) has been convicted of using the property, or allowing it to be used, for immoral or illegal purposes, or an arrestable offence committed in the property or in the locality.

Ground 15

The condition of the furniture in the property has got worse because it has been ill treated by the tenant or any other person living there.

Ground 16

The tenancy was granted because the tenant was employed by the landlord, or a former landlord, but he or she is no longer employed by the landlord.

Ground 17

The landlord was persuaded to grant the tenancy on the basis of a false statement knowingly or recklessly made by the tenant, or a person acting at the tenant's instigation.

Notice periods

The landlord must serve notice seeking possession of the property on the tenant before starting court proceedings. He or she must give the following amount of notice:

(a) for grounds 3, 4, 8, 10, 11, 12, 13, 15 or 17 – at least two weeks;

(b) for grounds 1, 2, 5, 6, 7, 9 and 16 – at least two months.

If the tenancy is on a contractual periodic or statutory periodic basis, the notice period must end on the last day of a tenancy period. The notice period must also be a least as long as the period of the tenancy, so that three months' notice must be given if it is a quarterly tenancy.

For ground 14 from 28 February 1997 – the landlord can start proceedings as soon as he or she has served notice.

Again, notice must be given before any court action can be taken ('Section 8' notice) – usually two weeks' notice, but sometimes two months' (see below). Notice must be in the prescribed form as set out by the Assured Tenancies and Agricultural Occupancies (Forms) Regulations 1997 (**www.opsi.gov.uk**).

If the circumstances justifying the grounds cited in the notice have not changed by the expiry of the notice period, County Court proceedings can be issued using form N5 'Claim form for possession of property' and N119 'Particulars of claim for possession (rented residential premises)'. Some of the grounds require the court to grant possession, some allow it discretion in the matter.

There is nothing to stop a landlord citing more than one of the grounds for requiring possession – ground 8 and ground 9 could be cited simultaneously, for example.

Accelerated Possession Procedure

In less complicated cases involving assured shorthold tenancies there is what is supposed to be a quicker method of gaining possession which may avoid the need for a court hearing. The 'Accelerated Possession Procedure' limits claims to possession and the cost of making the application and cannot be used, for example, to claim for rent arrears – although the small claims court can still be used for this.

The court will normally make its decision by looking at the written evidence provided by the landlord and the tenant – which means special care is needed in making sure all relevant evidence is included with the claim.

Accelerated possession procedures can be brought using form 5b: 'Claim for possession (accelerated procedure)'. The form and guidance on the procedure are available on the HM Court Service website **www.hmcourts-service.gov.uk**.

Conditions of Seeking Possession

During the fixed term of an assured or shorthold tenancy, the landlord can only seek possession if one of grounds 2, 8, 10 to 15 or 17 apply and the terms of the tenancy make provision for it to be ended on any of these grounds. When the fixed term of an assured tenancy ends, possession can be sought on any of the grounds.

When the fixed term of a shorthold tenancy ends, the landlord does not have to give any grounds for possession.

Before starting court proceedings for possession the landlord must serve notice allowing the periods set out in the above Act. If the tenancy is on a contractual periodic or statutory periodic basis, the notice period must end on the last day of a tenancy period (usually a month or sometimes three months, depending on the frequency of rental payments). The notice period must also be a least as long as the tenancy period, so that three months' notice must be given if the tenancy period is a quarterly, notwithstanding that the specified period is two months or less.

The exception is ground 14 – that the tenant, or someone living in or visiting the property has caused, or is likely to cause, a nuisance or annoyance to someone living in or visiting the locality; or the that tenant or someone living in or visiting the property been convicted of using the property, or allowing it to be used, for immoral or illegal purposes, or an arrestable offence committed in the property or in the locality. In such cases the landlord can start proceedings as soon as he has served notice.

A prior notice ground means that the landlord must have notified the tenant in writing before the tenancy started that he or she might seek possession on this ground (best done by inclusion of such notice in the tenancy agreement).

Evicting Squatters

Landlords may not turn out anybody living in their properties without a court order – and that includes squatters.

These are people who have entered and stayed living in a property without permission.

Even if they have not broken into the premises – which would be a crime in itself, although often difficult to prove if the property has been left empty for any length of time – squatting is a criminal offence (under the Criminal Justice and Public Order Act 1994, a copy of which can be downloaded from **www.opsi.gov.uk**). That does not mean that squatters do not have rights, or that they are any the easier to evict. Again, force must not be used. Unless friendly persuasion works, a court order will be required to regain possession.

> **"** Even if they have not broken into the premises squatting is a criminal offence. **"**

Courts are usually reluctant to make people homeless and local authorities are usually not inclined to advise people with nowhere to go to leave any accommodation until they absolutely have to. This means landlords who find themselves in the unfortunate position of having unwanted squatters in their property simply have to sit it out until the full legal niceties are observed.

The legal process

The legal process for evicting squatters involves obtaining an Interim Possession Order, usually from the County Court local to the property. The claim can be made against *persons unknown* and should be made within 28 days of first becoming aware of the squatters (or of the date you could reasonably be expected to have become aware of them). An interim order may not be sought against anybody who entered or remained on the premises with the consent of a person who, at the time consent was given, had an immediate right of possession (say, a tenant whose tenancy had not expired).

The squatters will have to be informed of the application, if necessary by fixing a notice to a door. According to HM Courts Service, decisions on applications for Interim Possession Orders are usually made within a few days. The relevant application forms and further advice can be obtained from the Courts Service website (**www.hmcourts-service.gov.uk** – search for 'squatters').

The effects of an interim possession order are serious and the Court will wish to protect the defendants' interests if the order is later set aside. So the landlord will be asked to undertake to allow the defendants back in and pay them damages should it later turn out that he or she was not entitled to the order, and not to let the premises to anyone else or damage them, or dispose of any of the defendants' possessions until the court makes a final decision on right to possession.

It is not a requirement that these undertakings be made, but the court will take a landlord's willingness to do so into account when deciding whether or not to grant an Interim Possession Order.

If an Interim Possession Order is obtained, it must be served on the occupants within 48 hours. After that the squatters must leave within 24 hours – if they do not they will be guilty of a criminal offence and the landlord can ask the police to arrest them. If they are convicted, they may be imprisoned, or fined, or both.

When applying for an interim possession order, the landlord should also make an application for a final order for possession, which will usually be made at a hearing shortly after the interim possession order has been made.

Full possession procedures

If, for some reason, it is not possible or appropriate to seek an Interim Possession Order, the position is not lost, but a full court hearing will have to be undertaken before the property can be claimed back and this will take longer.

The Ministry of Justice website (**www.justice.gov.uk**) has further information on all possession and interim possession claims (search for 'possession claims').

When squatters take over

Squatting is not the problem it once presented, but it does still cause serious problems for some landlords. This includes damage to their properties and void periods when no rent is coming in while they fight to get their properties back.

In the past, allowing squatters to live in property unchallenged proved even more serious for some local authorities that apparently lost track of properties they owned, or thought them uninhabitable. As a result people who had been allowed to live long enough unchallenged in such flats and houses were able to claim, and enforce, ownership rights.

One such squatter was Timothy Ellis, who having lived rent and council tax-free in a four bedroom Victorian terraced house in Brixton, south London, for 16 years, in 1999 persuaded the High Court that it should be his to sell.

Lambeth Council failed to prevent him from doing so because it had not asserted its ownership rights for the previous 12 years – the period then specified in the Statute of Limitations for claims to be effective.

The Council had previously lost a County Court hearing over ownership of the house, then valued at around £200,000.

Ellis was not the only squatter to gain so spectacularly from his unauthorised residence.

A year later Jack Blackburn, who also lived in Brixton, gained the ownership of his council flat after living there without permission for 13 years. He had moved in when there was fire damage which left it almost derelict. He changed the locks to his own and decorated the flat. After that he made continual improvements.

"The council didn't bother me for ten years and then realised that Brixton was an up-and-coming area and they could make money from doing the block up. I would have paid rent but they never asked," Blackburn was quoted as saying, after three Court of Appeal judges reversed a County Court eviction order.

The law was changed by the Land Registration Act 2002, which allows squatters such as Blackburn and Ellis fewer opportunities to gain ownership via "adverse possession" (possession without consent). Since this Act, registration of title is the primary factor in ownership.

Even so, squatters may still apply for ownership to be registered in their name (now after 10 years of adverse possession), although the registered owner can object. If he or she does so within the time allowed (65 working days) the Land Registry will reject the application. At this point the registered owner has two years to bring eviction proceedings against the squatter, otherwise he or she will be able to make another application. The Land Registry has published guidance about this in the form of the Land Registration Act 2002, Fact Sheet 2, which can be downloaded from **www.landregistry.gov.uk**.

11.

Local Housing Authorities

Enforcement of many of the laws, rules and regulations concerning private rented accommodation is in the hands of local authorities.

Although laws generally apply to the whole of England and Wales (Scotland has its own legal system and requirements in Northern Ireland also differ), the way in which they are applied can differ in detail from local authority to local authority (as do the amounts charged for landlord licences, for example). Landlords should be aware of the housing policies and housing priorities of the local authority or authorities responsible for locations in which they own rental property (these should be available via the relevant authorities' websites).

Responsibilities

Local authorities are responsible for implementing laws concerning:

- private rented sector housing standards
- landlord licensing
- local housing allowance
- private rented sector grants and subsidies
- management of empty properties.

Some local authorities also run landlord-accreditation schemes.

Duties

Local authority duties are taken care of by various departments or local offices:

- housing officers are local government officers with responsibilities for allocating social housing and dealing with antisocial behaviour

- planning officers have responsibility for planning permission applications and enforcement

- Building Control has responsibility for seeing building work complies with building regulations

- landlord licensing teams deal with licence applications and licence enforcement

- environmental health officers are local authority officers with responsibility for identifying and enforcing or coordinating enforcement of laws dealing with unfit or overcrowded private rental properties, with ensuring the suitability of HMO properties, and with illegal eviction and empty homes

- local Trading Standards offices have statutory responsibility for enforcing a raft of legislation, including consumer protection laws. Local Trading Standards offices can be found by postcode searches on **www.tradingstandards.gov.uk**.

Landlords will probably have most contact with local environmental health departments.

Enforcement Powers

Local authorities have various powers of entry and enforcement, made stronger by the Housing Act 2004.

Hazard remedies

Should they become aware of, or receive an official complaint of category-one (extreme) or category-two (severe) hazards within a property, the Act calls upon them to inspect that property. If category-one hazards are found to exist, there is a duty to take "appropriate enforcement action", and if category-two hazards are found, there is a power to take such action if deemed necessary (see Chapter 3, 'Suitable Properties').

This action could be serving: an improvement notice requiring works to remove the hazard; making a prohibition order debarring use of all or part of the property as a residential dwelling; serving a hazard awareness notice bringing attention to the hazard and recommending remedial action; taking emergency remedial action to remove an imminent danger; making an emergency prohibition order; or even making a demolition order.

If a council intends to take action concerning a fire hazard in an HMO or the common parts of a building containing flats, it has a duty to consult the local Fire and Rescue authority.

It is an offence not to comply with these legal notices and besides a fine, non-compliance could result in a court order for necessary work to be undertaken by the local authority at the owner's expense.

Licence breaches and takeovers

Local authorities also have power to step in when local licensing requirements have been breached. If a property should have been licensed but has not been, and there is no reasonable expectation that a licence will be granted in the near future, the local authority can issue an interim management order (IMO). Ownership of the property is not affected, but the local authority takes over the management, standing in the place of the landlord (see the government booklet 'Interim and Final Management Orders', **www.communities.gov.uk**).

The local authority will let the property as if it were the landlord, deal with tenants, collect the rent and pay all the outgoings for repairs, lettings costs and the like. It will pay the landlord the difference, if any, between the rental income and its costs. Authorities can also issue such orders when they intend to revoke landlord licences on certain grounds and there is no reasonable prospect that a new licence will be granted in the near future. Properties that do not need a licence are not entirely immune. On the authority of a Residential Property Tribunal (the body to which appeals against IMOs can be directed – **www.rpts.gov.uk**), local authorities can take over management of properties which are the source of anti-social behaviour about which the landlord is failing to take appropriate action.

Landlords can ask at any time for IMOs to be lifted. If a request is refused, an appeal can be made to the Residential Property Tribunal.

However, IMOs can also be followed (after due notification and consultation – and with right of appeal) by Final Management Orders (FMOs). These can last for as long as five years. Again the council stands in place of the landlords and accounts to him or her for any surplus income. Landlords have the right to ask at any time for an FMO to be lifted and, if refused, can appeal the decision.

Overcrowding and noise notices

Councils can take other action against those HMOs that do not require a licence. The Housing Act 2004 allows local authorities, where they consider there are too few rooms to accommodate everybody who lives or are likely to live at the premises, to issue overcrowding notices ordering the landlord to reduce the number of occupants or to prevent new tenants being accepted.

Any property can be subject to a noise abatement order if environmental health officers consider the level of noise from a property to be prejudicial to health or a nuisance. The notice could require the noisy activity to stop, demand steps to reduce the noise (such as insulation or volume control) or restrict the times of day that the noisy activity can take place. If the problem relates to the condition of the premises, the notice can be served on the landlord or owner of the premises. The person named on the notice has 21 days to challenge it in a magistrates' court, after which he or she can be fined for each day that the noise continues.

According to the Environmental Protection Act 1990, noise becomes a nuisance if unreasonable and significant level of noise causes significant and unreasonable interference with the use and enjoyment of a building. Where noise becomes excessive in volume and duration, or occurs at unreasonable times of the day, councils can investigate and assess whether or not the noise amounts to a statutory nuisance. Nuisance law is criminal law, and penalties on prosecution may include a fine or forfeiture of any seized noise-making equipment.

More likely, in the first instance at least, is an abatement notice. This is a legal document that requires the recipient to stop making unreasonable noise. It may also contain conditions to ensure that a nuisance does not occur in the future. Non-compliance with the requirements of an abatement notice is itself a criminal offence with fines of up to £5,000.

Empty dwellings

Councils can also take action to take control of and let out residential properties left empty for more than six months – the main homes of people temporarily living elsewhere for work or caring purposes are exempted, as are second homes and holiday homes, properties that are in the process of being sold or let, and properties that are going through probate.

Local authorities can only issue Empty Dwelling Management Orders with prior approval from a Residential Property Tribunal. Orders can be ended early if the owner decides to live in or sell the property.

Once an EDMO is in place the local authority concerned is responsible for any furniture remaining and must undertake any work needed to make a property habitable (recouping the costs from rental income).

Once a property is fit for habitation the local authority must seek permission from the owner for it to be occupied. If the owner is willing to allow it to be let, the authority may decide to return the property or to lease it from the owner, and charge him or her for the work done. But if the owner objects to letting the property, the local authority has the option to issue a final EDMO (if it does not, it must end the temporary EDMO). No further approval is needed from the RPT but the owner must be given 14 days to make representations. If the authority still goes ahead, the owner has the right of appeal.

Final EDMOs allow local authorities to take possession of a property for up to seven years, during which time they will let the property to whomever they consider appropriate. As before, local authorities must account to the owner for any net surplus from letting, after deducting costs.

For further details, see the government booklet 'Empty Dwelling Management Orders: Guidance for residential property owners', available to download from **www.communities.gov.uk**.

Fire safety

Trading Standards offices are responsible for enforcing legislation concerning the safety of goods supplied in rented accommodation. This includes the safety of gas and other appliances (and the requirement for annual gas safety certificates) and compliance with the Furniture and Furnishings (Fire) (Safety) Regulations 1988.

As *fire* is one of the 29 hazards identified by the Housing Health and Safety Rating System (HHSRS – listed in Chapter 3) landlords have a duty to assess the risk of fire in their rented properties and to provide appropriate measures to minimise that risk. Further, the Regulatory Reform (Fire Safety) Order 2005 (available from **www.opsi.gov.uk**) requires a written fire risk assessment as a condition of HMO licensing.

While local housing authorities are responsible, under the Housing Act 2004, for rented property licensing and for administering the HHSRS, Fire and Rescue authorities have the responsibility of enforcing the Fire Safety Order in the common areas of residential accommodation (other than single private dwellings). This means Fire and Rescue authorities have powers to inspect rented properties and to issue enforcement and prohibition notices where they deem them necessary.

LACORS (the Local Authorities Coordinators of Regulatory Services) has issued guidance on 'Housing – Fire Safety' outlining both fire safety requirements and how enforcement is shared between local authorities and fire and safety authorities. This can be downloaded from **www.lacors.gov.uk**.

Ignoring improvement orders can be costly

In 2009, Stratford magistrates fined a Newham landlord for ignoring improvement orders issued by his local council.

Found to have committed a serious breach of the Housing Act 2004, Kuldip Singh Minhas had to pay £3,750 in fines, plus a further £3,750 to meet council costs and £15 as a victim surcharge.

The magistrates discounted his claim that he was waiting for his tenant to move out before undertaking improvements to his property. Despite an improvement notice, he had made no attempt to contact or work with the council to put defects right.

Council officers had inspected Minhas' rented flat following a complaint from a tenant. They found it in a state of disrepair, with a number of rotten window and door frames. Water was leaking through the ceiling and a poorly installed skylight was also allowing moisture into the home.

The kitchen units and food preparation area were in very poor condition and the floor coverings throughout the flat were uneven and damaged. Council officers had additional concerns about the security of the property, with several doors lacking adequate locks.

The improvement notice served on Minhas cited a number of HHSRS category one and two hazards.

* * *

In 2010 a Carmarthenshire landlord was also fined for ignoring an improvement order.

As in Minhas' case, the local council had been alerted to defects by a tenant. And when inspectors visited the house owned and managed by Balasubramanian Pulendrathasan they found fire and food safety problems, inadequate personal hygiene

> **"** Landlords and their agents have a responsibility to provide healthy, safe and decent housing. **"**

facilities, and damp, mould growth and heat-loss problems.

Pulendrathasan was served with an improvement notice but further inspections revealed the required improvements had not been undertaken.

Pulendrathasan was offered assistance and advised on several occasions that if he could not manage the property it should be taken over by a relative or an agent. He was also warned about the consequences of failing to abide by the improvement notice and that if he was prosecuted he would not be considered a fit and proper person to manage an HMO.

When Pulendrathasan still did nothing he was prosecuted and fined £2,000, with £1,160 costs.

Carmarthenshire County Council executive board member for housing and public protection Councillor Hugh Evans said: "Landlords who act in this way will be prosecuted by the council. Both landlords and their agents have a responsibility to provide healthy, safe and decent housing."

Local Authority Grants

Local authorities are not only concerned with enforcement. Many support landlords by providing information and advice, sometimes training and/or landlord accreditation schemes, and also grants.

However, the general rule is that local authority grants are discretionary and subject to the availability of funds at the time of application. Landlords should check their own local authority's policies on the matter – the Directgov website (**www.direct.gov.uk**) has a search facility that enables landlords to go straight to the relevant page of the local authority for the town, street or postcode in which their rental property is situated.

Generally, improvement grants, if available, will be for a proportion of the costs of bringing a rental property up to HHSRS standards, with a maximum allowed for each property.

There are likely to be conditions relating to ownership, finance and other matters (such as the property being occupied by tenants who are not related to the landlord), a requirement for a current gas safety certificate and insurance cover. Grants will be repayable if the property is sold within a specified number of years. In some instances improvement grants are limited to members of the local landlords' accreditation scheme.

Landlord grants to cover a proportion of energy efficiency and security measures are also available from local authorities under the PLEASE scheme (Private Landlords Energy Award Scheme). Again, details need to be checked with the relevant local authority.

Empty Property Grants are also available from some local authorities – the Empty Homes Agency (**www.emptyhomes.com**) says there are usually conditions attached to this type of grant, such as making the property available for social housing for a fixed period.

Disabled tenants may be able to obtain a disabled facilities grant (there is a government leaflet explaining this that can be downloaded from **www.communities.gov.uk**). This is a means-tested grant to help with the costs of adapting a home to the needs of a disabled person – disabled tenants have the right to request alterations to property, other than structural changes, to meet their needs. Landlords may only refuse if they have reasonable grounds for doing so: for example, if the changes would prejudice the safety of other tenants. The changes will be at the disabled tenant's expense.

The grant is only available in England, Wales and Northern Ireland, although different rules apply in Wales (go to **new.wales.gov.uk**) and Northern Ireland (**www.nihe.gov.uk**).

Landlords may apply for the disabled facilities grant on behalf of disabled tenants. The maximum amount is £25,000 in Northern Ireland, £30,000 in England and £36,000 in Wales. The money can be used for adaptations to give disabled tenants better freedom of movement into and around the property and/or to provide essential facilities within it. Acceptable types of work include: widening doors and installing ramps; providing or improving access to rooms and facilities – for example, by installing a stair lift or providing a downstairs bathroom; improving or providing a heating system; and adapting heating or lighting controls to make them easier to use.

Tenants may also claim for warm front grants (**www.warmfront.co.uk**), towards the cost of insulation, of up to £3,500 (or £6,000 if oil central heating is involved). The scheme applies to England only; other schemes operate in Scotland, Wales and Northern Ireland (**www.eaga.com** for all).

Councils take action on empty homes

In April 2010 the then Under Secretary of State at the Department for Communities and Local Government, Ian Austin, told the House of Commons that since the 2004 Housing Act had given local authorities discretionary powers to take over the management of long-term privately owned empty homes 29 had done so.

Among them Norwich City Council had obtained six empty dwelling management orders (EDMOs). Most of the other authorities listed, including Staffordshire Moorlands District Council, had undertaken just one order.

Austin said EDMOs should only be considered as a last resort, where all other measures of investigation and negotiation have been exhausted and the local authority has been unable to persuade the owner to bring the property back into use. "In many cases the threat of an Empty Dwelling Management Order is sufficient to make owners take action," he claimed.

Staffordshire Moorlands District Council's EDMO gave it authority to break into an abandoned house that had been empty for years. Council officers were accompanied by police when they forced entry.

"Empty homes can cause a nuisance to a neighbourhood, attracting vandalism and vermin," commented councillor Andrew Hart, portfolio holder for housing and regeneration. He continued.

"We're committed to tackling the shortage of affordable housing in Staffordshire Moorlands by bringing empty houses back into use.

"We have wide ranging enforcement powers that we bring to bear on those owners who allow their property to remain empty and blight the local area."

Local Housing Allowance

Local housing allowance (the current form of housing benefit) is a means-tested payment made to low-income families in rented accommodation.

The amount of allowance paid is fixed by reference to the relevant *broad rental market areas* (see page 176) and household size. An explanatory booklet is available to download at **lha-direct.voa.gov.uk**. It is intended to reflect the *middle of the range* rental for a suitably sized property in the area. That size will depend upon the size of the household – allowing one bedroom per couple, plus one more for any other person over 10 (except children between 10 and 16 of the same sex are expected to be housed two to a room) and one more for any two children under the age of 10.

For single claimants under 25 years old there is a *shared* rate of LHA. This rate also applies to single people over 25 and couples with no other occupiers who choose to live in shared accommodation.

Local housing allowance rates are set by the Rent Service. The website LHA Direct (**lha-direct.voa.gov.uk**) has a local housing allowance calculator by local authority area.

LHA is paid to claimants, not to landlords. The principle is that tenants negotiate the actual rent to be paid, make up any difference or keep any excess up to a maximum of £15 per week.

Tenants can claim LHA as soon as they have a rental agreement in place. An 'A to Z' of local councils can be found on the LHA Direct webiste.

According to government advice on LHA, it is up to tenants to pay their rent to their landlords. If they do not, they may be taken to court and evicted from the property.

Effective from January 2009, local housing allowance was linked to rents payable in broad rental market areas (BRMAs). These reference rents are those for properties in areas within which a tenant of the dwelling could reasonably be expected to live given the facilities and services available for health care, education, recreation, personal banking and shopping, and taking account of the distance of travel, by public and private transport, to and from those facilities and services.

To be used for determining reference rents for the purposes of setting LHA, BRMAs must encompass residential premises of a variety of types, including premises held on a variety of tenures, including privately rented residential premises. The mix must be such that, in the rent officer's opinion, the local reference rents for tenancies in the area are representative of the rents that a landlord might reasonably be expected to obtain in that area.

The reference rents determined for each BRMA can be checked on the website **lha-direct.voa.gov.uk**.

Pitfalls and positives

Housing benefit was a difficulty for landlords because it was often paid only after considerable delay. It was, or could be, paid directly to landlords, so at least landlords could be reasonably sure of receiving payment eventually. Against this, if tenants' circumstances changed or they had incorrectly claimed, leading to an overpayment of housing benefit, landlords were required to make repayments.

The new system is equally controversial since the allowance is paid to tenants who by definition will be coping on low incomes, so that there may be great temptation sometimes to hold back some or all of the rent. This means landlords accepting tenants who need to rely on local housing allowance may be taking on tenants with poor credit ratings and no guarantee that the allowance will come their way.

Against this, many landlords have no difficulties with such tenants and have the option to seek guarantors and, if necessary, to pursue tenants who fall behind with rent for payment via the Small Claims Court. It is possible for the circumstances of any tenant to change during a tenancy, so that he or she becomes a local housing allowance claimant.

This points to treating prospective tenants who will rely on LHA in the same way as any other tenants – making the same credit checks, taking the same precautions and making a rental decision on business principles.

This will become increasingly pertinent given the coalition government's conclusion that housing benefits are out of control and its promise to introduce a package of reforms that it says will cut the annual predicted cost of housing benefits by almost £2bn (or 9%) within five years.

As noted above, housing allowance rates are currently set locally according to family needs – which can be for up to five bedrooms, based on the middle of the range of rents (the median) in each broad rental market area. But from April 2011 the rates will no longer be based on the median of BRMA rents but effectively on roughly 60% of the average (the 30th percentile of rents, as the government puts it).

What is more, housing benefit is to be capped. There will no longer be a five bedroom category, and the allowance for a four bedroom property will not be allowed to top £400 a week. The top rate for a one bedroom property will be £250, two bedroom £290, and the allowance for a three bedroom property will be £340.

This will mean there will be an end to the £2,000 a week that the government says is paid to some claimants in some parts of London.

There is more. LHA claimants will no longer be able to pocket the first £15 each week of any saving they make by renting a property for less than the allowance they receive. Also, from 2013, out of work tenants who have claimed job seeker's allowance for more than 12 months will have their housing benefits cut by 10% – as an incentive to do more to get back into work.

Recognising that the transition is likely to cause hardship, the government said it will triple its contribution to local authority funding for discretionary housing payments. This is currently £20m a year, and will increase to £30m in 2011/12 and then to £60m a year from 2012/13. This is comparatively small beer in relation to the current £20bn annual cost of housing benefit (£14bn paid to people of working age), not to mention the £25bn that the government says housing benefit would have cost in 2015/16 had changes not been made.

Taken overall, the government says the changes "will provide a fairer and more sustainable housing benefit scheme by taking steps to ensure that people on benefit are not living in accommodation that would be out of the reach of most people in work, creating a fairer system for low income working families and for the taxpayer. It will avoid the present situation where housing benefit recipients are able to live in very expensive properties in areas that most working people supporting themselves would have no prospect of being able to afford."

Under the new regime, local housing allowance claimants can expect to see the amounts they receive go down by an average of £12 per week. Some, of course, will see the amount go down by very much more.

The changes will apply to new claimants from the date they come into effect and to existing claimants from the anniversary of their claim – unless in the meantime they have a change of circumstances which requires their local authority to *redetermine* their claim sooner.

What these reforms mean is that people receiving housing benefit may not be able to live in expensive city centres, "but the same applies to most working families who do not receive benefit," said the government

Clearly landlords will have to reassess the potential market for their properties. If there is going to be less support for the rental of larger and more expensive city centre accommodation, demand is likely to reflect this – meaning rental interest and property prices for not so large properties in outlying residential areas are likely to come off not quite so badly. Landlords targeting the HB market might have to look again at their property portfolios.

Landlord attitudes to housing benefit tenants

In May 2009 the research company BDRC reported that, when asked what would make them more inclined to let to housing benefit tenants, 31% of landlords said it would be "abandoning the policy of paying benefits directly to tenants".

But 17% – one-in-six – said nothing would encourage them to take housing benefit tenants.

Even so, the firm said more landlords had in fact taken on tenants claiming housing benefit – in fact, the number had more than doubled, from 9% in the last quarter of 2008 to 20% in the first quarter of 2009. One reason was that more tenants were under increased financial pressure and unable to pay their rents, so there were simply fewer potential tenants not claiming the allowance.

This was despite, said the research, "a number of factors deterring more private landlords from considering benefit claimants as viable tenants". The top three reasons given were: not trusting them to look after the property (24%), a previous bad experience (15%), and not trusting them to pay the rent (10%).

One landlord told BDRC: "New DSS [Department of Social Services – referring to LHA claimants] tenants get their rental money paid directly to them – not the landlords – and as a landlord you do not see it. It was a very bad move by the government to change this policy."

12.

Taxation

As renting property is a business, the profits from that business are taxable.

Landlords are generally liable to three types of tax: income tax (or corporation tax) on net rental income; capital gains tax on profits from buying, holding and selling property; and VAT.

Income Tax

Letting residential property is treated as running a business whether there is one property involved or one hundred. This means that tax is payable on the *net profit* – rental income less expenses incurred in the rental business and certain allowances (explained below).

Landlords who run their letting business via a limited company have to pay corporation tax; those who retain personal ownership of their properties must pay income tax.

Special allowances

In arriving at their taxable rental income, landlords are permitted to deduct some special allowances. For example, when letting a furnished room within his or her own home, the Rent a Room scheme allows the landlord to receive gross income – including any charge for meals, laundry or other services – of £4,250 tax free (correct as at June 2009 – see **www.direct.gov.uk**).

Landlords who choose not to use the Rent a Room scheme can claim the expenses of letting, including a proportion of mortgage interest, against rental income in the normal way. The normal way is to declare income less the expenses of letting and a proportion of mortgage interest.

Another special landlord allowance (not available to landlords taking advantage of the Rent a Room scheme) is the Landlords Energy Saving Allowance (LESA). This permits both private and corporate landlords to claim up to £1,500 for each rented property as an offset against their taxable income for the installation of energy saving improvements, including loft, cavity wall and floor insulation, upgraded heating systems and draft proofing.

In the case of fully furnished property, which HMRC says is property "capable of normal occupation without the tenant having to provide their own beds, chairs, tables, sofas and other furnishings, cooker, etc,"(see 'Furnished residential property: wear and tear allowance', available from **www.hmrc.gov.uk**), there is a wear and tear allowance available to the landlord equivalent to 10% of the *net rent* from the furnished letting. Landlords have the option to disregard this allowance and instead set against rental income the cost of replacing contents (but not of their initial purchase) when renewal becomes necessary.

If a landlord with both furnished and unfurnished property claims the wear and tear allowance, this must be calculated on the basis of the net rent from furnished properties only. The net rent is defined as rent less any charges paid by the landlord that would normally be borne by a tenant (for example, council tax or water and sewerage rates).

The wear and tear allowance is intended to cover appliances and furnishings, not fixtures such as baths, wash basins, toilets and central heating systems. This means that whether or not the wear and tear allowance is claimed, the net cost (cost less the proceeds of the sale of the fixtures being replaced) of replacing such fixtures can usually be claimed against rental income.

Expenses

When completing tax returns, the expenses that landlords can deduct from their letting income to arrive at a net taxable amount include the following (provided they have been incurred solely for the purposes of running the letting business):

- interest (but not capital repayments) on loans and mortgages used for the letting business

- bank charges on an account used for the business

- buildings and contents insurance

- utility bills paid by the landlord

- council tax on rental property paid by the landlord

- the cost of maintenance and repairs (but not improvements), including replacement of appliances and furnishings (but not if the 10% wear and tear allowance is claimed), and of fixtures

- services such as cleaning and gardening

- advertising costs

- the cost of Gas Safety and other certificates and licences

- training courses and subscriptions to relevant magazines

- other direct costs of the letting business such as phone calls, stationery, travelling, loss of rent insurance cover, the cost of credit checks, debt recovery and associated legal costs

- any rent, ground rent, or service charges paid by the landlord

- any letting agent's fees

- legal fees for lets of a year or less, or for renewing a lease for less than 50 years

- accountants' fees.

Costs incurred prior to receiving any rents (up to seven years before) can be claimed, provided they are for the purposes of the letting business and are not *capital* in nature (costs of acquiring and improving the property) and are such that they would be allowable had rent already been received. So, repairs to a property would be allowable, but the cost of improvements (often a fine line) would not (although the cost of improvements are deductible from any capital gain when the property is sold – capital gains tax is covered in a later section in this chapter).

When an existing property is first introduced into a letting business, the tax rules allow the property to be refinanced and tax relief to be obtained even if the proceeds of the loan are not used for the letting business. Interest on loans used to finance the letting business, including the purchase of property, are allowable even if secured against property which is not part of the business.

Landlords whose usual place of abode is outside the UK still have to pay tax on their UK letting income. Under the non-resident landlords (NRL) Scheme (**www.hmrc.gov.uk**), tax at the standard rate must be deducted and accounted for either by the non-resident landlord's UK letting agent or by his or her tenants (tenants who make payments of less than £100 per week to non-resident landlords do not have to deduct and account for tax unless they have been told to do so by the Revenue's Charities Assets and Residency office (CAR), but there is no similar concession for letting agents).

Non-resident landlords – whose UK tax affairs are up to date, or have had no UK tax obligations before, or do not expect to be liable to UK income tax, or are not liable to pay UK tax because they are Sovereign Immunes (these are generally foreign heads of state, governments or government departments) – can apply to receive their rent with no tax deducted.

If HMRC grants the application it will send a notice of approval to the non-resident landlord, and a separate notice to the letting agent or tenants named in the application form, authorising payment of rent to the non-resident landlord without deducting tax. Authority to pay rent to a non-resident landlord with no tax deducted is generally backdated to the beginning of the quarter in which HMRC receives the application.

Similar rules apply to non-resident companies.

Further guidance and relevant forms are available from **www.hmrc.gov.uk**.

Annual tax return

Whether or not their entire income comes from rental income, and whether or not they are also employed full or part-time, landlords with rental income and/or allowable expenses should complete an annual tax return declaring their income (even if HMRC does not request a return, landlords have a legal responsibility to declare their income if this gives rise to tax liabilities).

If the business is run as a partnership, say between a husband and wife, each partner should make an annual tax return, each declaring their share of both income and expenses. Businesses run as limited companies will be required to complete an annual corporation tax return.

There are different types of personal tax return containing different supplementary pages, which have to be completed depending on circumstances. If total income from letting (before deduction of expenses) is less than £15,000, only a shorter return may be required in which only the total of expenses need be included; if it is £15,000 or above, a longer return including pages specific to letting income will be required, including a breakdown of expenses. HMRC has an explanation of the process on **www.hmrc.gov.uk**.

Returns should be completed even where the letting business is making losses, since these can be carried forward and set against future profits.

Landlords who have unused personal tax allowances can set these against their taxable income from letting.

Be aware that there are also deadlines for submitting tax returns, and penalties and interest charges on late submissions.

Tax is a complicated subject with detailed rules for many different circumstances. Landlords with significant rental income should consider appointing a tax accountant to give advice on minimising their tax liability and completing necessary returns.

Whether or not a tax accountant is employed, landlords must keep adequate accounting records to be able to satisfy HMRC if required. These records should include cash books detailing all receipts and payments, including drawings, invoices and copies of any receipts given. This is the subject of chapter 13.

HM Revenue and Customs' 'Property Income Manual' can be accessed at **www.hmrc.gov.uk**.

Capital Gains Tax (CGT)

Landlords must pay capital gains tax on the profits they make when selling off their investment properties (tax is payable on the net sales proceeds after legal and other selling costs, less the costs of buying the property in the first place, and less the cost of any improvements).

As from 23 June 2010, standard rate taxpayers pay 18% on their capital gains realised after that date but higher rate taxpayers pay 28%.

However, since capital gains are added to income to determine whether or not the higher rate of income tax applies (for the tax year 2010/2011 it kicks in when taxable income less personal allowance exceeds £37,400), only standard rate taxpayers with relatively small capital gains are likely to be eligible for the 18% rate. Most landlords will find they have to pay 28% tax on the gains made on their properties.

Individuals are taxed on capital gains at a rate derived from treating the taxable gains as if they were part of their income. Provided they earn less than £100,000 a year, taxpayers have a personal allowance of (for 2010-2011 – tax years run from 6 April to 5 April following) £6,475 (higher amounts apply to older taxpayers: £9,490 for those aged between 65 and 74, and £9,640 for those aged 75 and over). After this the first £2,440 of 2010-2011 savings income is taxed at 10%, and the next £34,960 of income at 20%. If there is no savings income, the whole of the first £37,400 income is taxed at 20%. After this taxpayers become *higher rate* taxpayers, paying 40% on earnings between £37,401 and £150,000, and 50% on earnings above this amount.

So in practical terms most people become higher rate taxpayers when their earnings exceed £6,475 (their personal allowance) plus £37,400 (the upper end of the 20% tax rate band) or £43,875.

When it comes to capital gains, there is (for 2010-2011) an annual tax exempt amount of £10,100 to deduct. Once this is taken off, any remaining amount of gain is taxed at 18% or 28%. Taking the simple case of entitlement to the 20% tax band, if total taxable income plus taxable capital gain is less than £43,875, then the whole gain is taxed at 18%. If the total taxable income plus taxable gain exceeds £43,875 then the amount of the gain which brings income up to the £43,875 mark is taxed at 18% and the balance at 28%. If taxable income already exceeds £43,875, the whole of the taxable capital gain is taxed at 28%.

There is an *entrepreneurs* relief that allows the first £1m of gains on disposals of trading businesses to be taxed at 10%. Property letting businesses, other than furnished holiday lettings businesses, are specifically excluded from this.

More on all of this is available from the HMRC website at **www.hmrc.gov.uk**.

Exemptions and concessions

Partners are taxed on their share of capital gains and each has an annual exemption. So a married couple in business partnership would between them have a total annual exemption of £20,200 (for 2010/2011, with a promise from the Chancellor that it will thereafter rise with inflation).

Unfortunately, although HMRC regards rental property as a 'capital' item, it does not regard it as a *business asset* for the purpose of some reliefs that might otherwise apply – namely roll over relief and entrepreneurs' relief. So these are not available to landlords.

However, there are concessions for landlords whose rental property has previously been their principal private residence. In such circumstances gains arising in the first three years after moving out are not taxable (they are considered an extension of the period in which the property was occupied as the landlord's principal private residence – and most capital gains on the sale of private residences are exempt from CGT).

If a property that was formerly a principal private residence is sold after having been let out for more than three years, any capital gains must be apportioned between the period of use as a private residence (plus three years) and the total time owned. Only the first is exempt from CGT.

Anybody owning more than one property can, within two years of each purchase of an additional property, write to HMRC to nominate one as his or her principal residence. If no nomination is made, the matter will be decided by HMRC on the evidence available, such as where mail is usually directed, and the address used for your entry on the electoral roll. Married and civil partnership couples have to agree on the nomination they make (by both signing the HMRC notification) and, unless formally separated, may between them have only one principal private residence at a time. Unmarried couples may each own a home that qualifies as their principal residence.

Landlords moving out of their principal residence in order to let it out may also claim *private letting relief*. Up to £40,000 may be claimed, and as with the annual capital gains exemption, both a husband and wife or civil partners who are also partners in the property and the letting may each claim this amount.

Again, it is always best to take professional advice.

HMRC recommends that property owners keep detailed information about their properties including: contracts for the purchase, sale, lease or exchange of the property; any documentation relating to properties obtained as gifts or inheritances; details of any properties that have been given away or put into a trust; copies of any valuations taken into account in CGT calculations of gains or losses; bills, invoices or other evidence of payment records such as bank statements and cheque stubs for purchase and improvement costs, buying costs and sale proceeds and costs. "It would also be sensible to keep correspondence with buyers or sellers leading up to the sale of the property," it says.

HMRC has a page on its website devoted to: 'How to calculate capital gains on property' – **www.hmrc.gov.uk**

Rather than CGT, companies have to pay corporation tax on capital gains (in corporation tax rules, known as *chargeable gains*). The rules for calculation and the amount payable therefore differ – for example, personal allowances and reliefs do not apply; see below.

Corporation Tax

In law a limited company is a separate entity to its owners. And it is the company, and not the individual owners, who must pay tax on company profits and any capital gains it makes. That tax is corporation tax.

(This, of course, does not mean the owners do not have to pay tax also. They are assessed on the money they draw out of the company in the form of salaries, fees and dividends.)

The amount of corporation tax that companies are obliged to pay is based on the gains, both profits and capital gains, revealed in the company's statutory accounts – the accounts that must be drawn up and filed at Companies House each year. In fact, if the company is a small company and only files what are known as *abbreviated accounts*, HMRC will also require additional figures.

However, whether or not additional information is required by HMRC, the profit included in the statutory accounts will not coincide exactly with taxable gains. This is because some expenses incurred by companies – entertainment expenses, for example – are not allowable as a deduction from taxable income. Also, HMRC has its own way of making allowance for use of company assets such as cars and computers. Whereas statutory accounts will contain a charge known as *depreciation* (usually a set percentage of the cost of each asset), corporation tax calculations must substitute what are known as *capital allowances* in place of depreciation. There will be a difference, although probably not a huge difference.

Also, a company's accounts may cover a different period from its corporation tax accounting period, although the two usually coincide. If they do not, there will be further adjustments to make.

There are currently two rates of corporation tax, depending on the level of taxable profits. The small profits rate for taxable profits of up to £300,000 is 21% for corporation tax accounting periods starting on or after 1 April 2010 and 20% for those starting after 1 April 2011. The comparable *full rates* applicable to profits in excess of £300,000 are 28% and 27%. What is known as *marginal relief* applies for profits between £300,000 and £1.5m so that the effective percentage of profits in this band will always be less than the full rate.

Note that when it comes to capital gains, companies are not entitled to an annual tax exemption. However, they do benefit from an indexation allowance which is designed to remove the effects of inflation from any gain. The amount of allowance is calculated on the basis of tables published by HMRC reflecting movements in the Retail Price Index (an official index of inflation) since the asset or assets were bought. There are monthly figures to refer to going back many years.

Salaries paid to owner-directors should be taxed under PAYE (pay as you earn) income tax rules, with the company deducting tax and National Insurance according to official tables which spread personal allowances over the tax year. Dividends paid to owner-directors out of taxed company profits come with a tax credit (equal to one-ninth of the amount received – in other words, for income tax purposes the recipient is deemed to have had 10% deducted from a notional gross amount). If you receive dividends you will have to declare these as income in your annual tax return, even assuming the whole of your personal allowance has been used up by other income, but there will be nothing extra to pay on the first £2,440 (2010-2011) of taxable dividends, since the applicable income tax rate is 10%. There will also be no National Insurance for the company to pay – which would not be the case if the same amount were paid as salary.

When disposing of shares in a company, owner-directors could well meet the various conditions for entrepreneurs' relief mentioned above. If both husband and wife are owner-directors of the company, both could qualify for the relief up to an upper limit of £1m of gains each.

For further information, see the official HMRC website, **www.hmrc.gov.uk**, which has various help sheets.

Value Added Tax (VAT)

Rental of residential property (other than holiday lets) is exempt from VAT in the UK. No matter the amount of rental income, unless they have vatable income from other sources, landlords are not required to register for VAT, or permitted to add VAT to their rents.

Exempt has a special meaning in VAT terms. Some types of goods have no VAT added (*zero-rated* supplies) although the VAT registered traders who sell them can still claim back any VAT charged on business costs and expenses. *Exempt* means VAT can neither be charged nor reclaimed. So VAT on landlord expenses is simply an addition to costs.

Should the need arise, further information about VAT rules can be obtained from **www.hmrc.gov.uk**.

The idea behind VAT is that businesses above a certain size (currently with annual turnover in excess of £70,000) must become VAT registered traders (by registering as such with HMRC) and thereafter charge VAT on the goods they sell. The amount charged is passed over to HMRC (usually quarterly) less the VAT element of goods and services the business has had to buy. So because VAT registered traders effectively claim back all the VAT they pay, it is only unregistered and VAT exempt customers who actually bear the cost of the tax.

The actual rate of VAT charged varies between 0% and 17.5% (to be increased to 20% from January 2011). Text books, children's clothing and many food items carry 0% VAT. Electricity has VAT charged at 5% and most other items 17.5%

VAT registered traders that sell mainly zero-rated goods are likely to pay more out in VAT than they charge – in which case they can claim the excess back from HMRC. However, exempt services, such as banking, do not charge or collect VAT from customers, but neither may they claim back the VAT they have paid on supplies – VAT is simply a cost to them. This is the position that applies to landlords.

13.

Record Keeping

Having accurate and easily accessible records is important to landlords for a number of reasons. These include:

- satisfying the tax authorities

- satisfying licensing and other authorities

- being able to prove compliance with statutory requirements – such as those for energy performance certificates, gas safety certificates, purchase of furniture that complies with fire safety regulations, and protection of tenant deposits

- keeping track of who owes what to whom – rents, agent's fees, repair bills and the like

- assessing the performance of the rental business and each of its rental properties.

Landlords will also want to know in detail the contents of each of their properties.

The above implies a need for both an adequate accounting system and also an archive of important documents.

If you let out property, you'll have to keep records of your income and expenses for at least six years – whatever type of letting it is. HM Revenue & Customs can ask to see supporting information for your figures at any point during this time.

Even though you can't claim expenses when you use the Rent a Room scheme, landlords using the scheme would still be well advised to keep proper records.

ff If you let out property, you'll have to keep records of your income and expenses for at least six years – whatever type of letting it is. **JJ**

All landlords should keep records of rent received and expenses paid, so as to be able to work out the profit on which they will have to pay tax. These can be kept in the form of physical books or as computer records. There are a number of proprietary software packages designed for landlords with few or a large number of properties (packages such as Rentman and Landlord Manager). For a list, consult **www.residentiallandlord.co.uk**. In any case, the information recorded should include:

- rental income – rent charged and received, with a separate note of any service or additional charges, the dates of each tenancy, and the names of tenants

- allowable expenses – including letting agents' fees, accountants' fees and legal fees, buildings and contents insurance, property loan interest, maintenance and repair costs, any professional cleaning costs, any utility bills paid, any ground rent or service charges, any council tax, and advertising costs and other direct costs

- capital costs – including the initial cost of property and contents, legal and other costs (such as stamp duty) associated with initial costs, plus improvement costs.

To back up these records landlords should keep receipts, invoices and bank statements – separating between their business and personal affairs.

Records should also include copies of any contracts, including maintenance and other contracts, copies of tenancy agreements, guarantees, deeds, leases, insurance policies and certificates, licences, correspondence with agents and correspondence with and notices from council and other authorities.

Businesses run via limited companies have additional accounting responsibilities. They must file annual statutory accounts (those drawn up in accordance with Companies Act requirements) at Companies House. These must show a *true and fair* view of the current position and, except in the case of the smallest companies, of profits and losses. Directors also have responsibility for ensuring records show, at any given moment, the company's assets, its liabilities, and its income and expenditure. Records must also show stock held at the financial year end.

HMRC requires that companies keep, for corporation tax purposes, up to date, complete and easily accessible records of:

- annual accounts, including a profit and loss statement and balance sheet

- bank statements and paying-in slips

- cash and petty cash transactions

- purchases and sales

- invoices (in the case of rental companies, rent demands)

- orders and deliveries; and

- relevant business correspondence.

Tenant information

Copies of the information that has to be provided to tenants should be kept. This includes:

- a current gas safety certificate

- a current energy performance certificate

- details of how and where each tenant's deposit has been protected.

Landlords are only required to provide rent books if the rent is payable weekly. If required the rent book must then by law contain, among other things, the name and address of the landlord, the rent payable and letting terms. Copies should be kept.

Disputes can and do arise between landlords and tenants, so landlords should be careful to keep records of all dealings with tenants both during and for some time after the tenancy has ended – to be absolutely safe, for six years (the time frame embodied in various laws limiting liability) – but certainly until after the matters of the return or otherwise of a deposit and any other possible claim or counter-claim have been resolved.

Such records should include any application form completed by the tenant, all correspondence with the tenant – including email and text messages – inventory records, and personal details such as next of kin, employer, NI number and copies of driving licences and passports, if taken, and of credit checks.

Holding such personal data brings landlords within the realms of the data protection regime – meaning they are likely to have to register as a *data controller* with the Information Commissioner's Office. This can be done online at **www.ico.gov.uk**, which also has a self-assessment guide to confirm whether or not registration is required. Not registering when it is a requirement to do so is a criminal offence.

The Data Protection Act requires that personal information should be kept secure and should only be kept for as long as is necessary for the purpose for which it was collected. *Data subjects*, those whose personal information it is, have the right to a copy of anything held on a computer on payment of a fee to the holder of the information (usually £1). All this is explained in more detail on the Information Commissioner's website (**www.ico.gov.uk** – also search at the site for 'Data Protection Good Practice Note, Disclosing information about tenants').

Landlord lost tenants' files

Orbit Heart of England Housing Association was in 2009 forced to give the Information Commissioner's Office a formal undertaking to sharpen up its data handling after it had lost tenant files during an office move. They had been left in a filing cabinet that had been sold second hand.

No inventory of files had been made prior to the move so staff were initially uncertain how many files should have been received at the new office. Eventually it was concluded that 57 paper files containing personal data had gone missing. Of these, 42 files were recovered, but 15 containing significant amounts of personal data about each tenant and, in some cases, members of their families remained missing. Some information contained details of ethnicity and physical or mental health.

Although the housing association had taken immediate steps to investigate the loss, the episode amounted to a breach of the Data Protection Act, the Information Commissioner's Office concluded.

As soon as it discovered that the information had been lost, Orbit contacted the tenants concerned. It also introduced a new procedure for future office moves and reported the incident to the ICO. It cooperated fully with the subsequent investigation.

Sally-Anne Poole, Head of Enforcement and Investigations at the ICO, said the incident "highlights the importance of ensuring correct procedures are in place when moving files containing people's personal details. These files included sensitive personal information which was compromised and it is concerning that 15 of these files are still missing."

Housing associations are in the main those independent bodies that now run what was once known as council housing but is now more generally called social housing – lower cost housing that can be rented long term. Most are not-for-profit organisations (that is to say they are not run to make a commercial profit, simply to pay their way). Many manage properties transferred to them from local councils and continue to work closely with them to meet local housing needs.

Most housing associations provide a range of housing, sometimes including accommodation designed for older, disabled or other more needy tenants.

Nearly all housing associations are regulated by the Tenant Services Authority, which ensures their housing stocks meet acceptable standards (the TSA has a website with more about this – go to portal.tenantservicesauthority.org). Housing association income is derived from rents and from government support for acquiring new homes.

Eight principles to follow

Anyone who processes personal information must comply with eight principles, which make sure that personal information is:

1. fairly and lawfully processed
2. processed for limited purposes
3. adequate, relevant and not excessive
4. accurate and up to date
5. not kept for longer than is necessary
6. processed in line with your rights
7. secure
8. not transferred to other countries without adequate protection.

14.

Insurance

Risks that are known and can be calculated can be covered by insurance. The logic is that if the outcome of some unwanted event is likely to be so damaging financially that the cost cannot easily be covered from regular income, then it is better to pay a smaller monthly or annual amount which ensures the eventuality can be met should the worst happen rather than simply to hope that it will not.

Of course, the decision will rarely be that simple. Whether it is worth taking out insurance will depend on the likelihood of loss and its possible size, the cover being offered, the extent to which the landlord is prepared or required by the insurer to bear a proportion of the risk, and the cost of the cover.

As insurance companies have differing assessments of different risks, different policies towards different geographical areas and/or types of rental property and tenants, and different priorities, it will always pay to shop around. Before doing so landlords should consider the cover they believe to be essential and that which simply could be worth arranging if offered at a reasonable price. Packaged landlord insurance policies may include elements that, given the landlord's circumstances, may not be required. There are also likely to be optional elements, some of which might be essential. Packages may appear similar but in fact differ in various ways from company to company.

Useful and Essential Cover

Forms of cover which some landlords have found worthwhile or essential include:

Property insurance

Property insurance will more than likely be a requirement of any buy-to-let mortgage. Cover should be for rental property specifically (relying on a standard household property without informing the insurance company that the property is let might negate the cover) and can include cover against fire, storm, theft, flood, accidental damage, malicious damage, terrorist attack and subsidence. Landlords should be sure that any insurance policy covers all the property risks they consider important. They should also make sure cover is adequate, remembering that it is the building that is being insured, not the land and the building. Rebuilding costs are likely to be less than the current market value of the property.

Alternative accommodation

If a rental property becomes uninhabitable for some reason (say, flooding), it is the landlord's duty to provide tenants with alternative accommodation. *Alternative accommodation* cover will protect against the additional costs arising from this eventuality. Landlords should check the extent of cover, limitations on the amounts payable and restrictions (such as type of property, location and required precautions).

Unoccupied property insurance

Most property insurance does not provide cover when buildings are left unoccupied for any length of time – say longer than three weeks. If this is a possibility, separate cover may need to be arranged. Restrictions are likely to apply. Prudent landlords will make sure their tenancy agreements make it a condition not to leave the property empty for a period which coincides with that specified in the insurance policy and will also make sure that the agreement includes *abandonment* clauses allowing them to take action should a tenant simply quit the property without warning.

Contents insurance

In this context, contents insurance covers landlord's contents, including furniture, furnishings and appliances. Tenants generally have to insure their own possessions separately. Again, it is important to make sure that the declared value is adequate – otherwise the landlord will be considered part self-insurer and will not receive a full payout should a claim arise. Also, it is usually the original cost of items that is insured rather than current value, although some insurers offer *new-for-old* cover.

Loss of rent

Loss of rent cover is intended to provide cover should a property remain empty for any length of time (void periods). The amount of cover will be restricted, the start date of payments probably delayed until the property has been empty for a period, and the number of weeks' cover limited. Landlords should be sure to check the extent of the cover being offered and the restrictions that apply.

Rent guarantee

This is protection against tenant default. Generally it will not apply for one, two, or three months while, in order to claim, landlords will have to be able to show that they have obtained proper credit checks, taken up references, and confirmed the identity of tenants, and that they have done all that is reasonable to avoid loss of rent (issuing appropriate reminders and notices in good time).

Landlord's legal liability

Landlords are liable for tenant and third party injuries that can be linked to the condition of their property at the time. The possibility of a claim arising might be remote, but, if one should arise, the sum involved might well be substantial. Landlord's legal liability provides cover, often to the extent of millions of pounds, for this risk.

Contents liability cover

Similarly, substantial claims and liability can arise from faulty contents. Contents liability cover (which can be wrapped up in general landlord's liability cover) will take care of this. Landlords should check restrictions and requirements including any maintenance records.

Legal expenses

This is often an optional extra in landlord insurance policies. If taken out, the cover is likely to be fixed at an annual maximum amount. Legal expenses cover can pay for pursuit of rent arrears, eviction of tenants, recovery of dilapidations, or claims against guarantors, as well as personal claims arising from renting – such as a claim for damages arising from injury. Having legal expenses cover can be helpful in that it allows landlords to take legal measures (for example, in disputes and possession proceedings) when the costs involved might otherwise make it impractical. Some insurers will include a legal helpline, which can be a great benefit, but landlords should check the extent of cover offered and any limitations or restrictions imposed.

Disclosure

It is important, when arranging insurance, to make full disclosure of circumstances. This way the insurer can better assess the risk, and there is less likelihood of an argument with the insurance company should a claim arise.

Among the disclosures asked for are likely to be the type of property (age and suitability) and type of tenants. Landlords should be aware that some insurance companies will place restrictions on both (for example, no listed buildings, no houses in multiple occupation, no student tenants, no asylum seeker tenants, or no tenants reliant on local housing allowance). Other companies may specialise in one or the other, which is why it is important to shop around.

Properties at Risk

England's Fire and Rescue Services attended 39,000 house fires in the year to March 2009, the Fire Statistics Monitor reported. Some 32,000 were put down as accidental.

Although that was fewer than the previous year, the Association of British Insurers had reported that the cost of fire damage to homes was increasing – £408m in 2008, an increase of 17% on the previous year.

Aviva property risk manager, Allister Smith, said fire damage to unoccupied and unfinished properties was a major concern for insurers. "Each year there are around 9,000 fires in empty buildings. If a vacant property is not regularly inspected, re-secured and repaired as required, an escalation in the frequency and size of incidents can be expected. This can also result in total destruction of the building."

Meanwhile, Endsleigh Insurance Services' 'Homes Report 2009', based on household theft claims over the previous year, named the top three riskiest UK towns for household theft as London, Nottingham and Bristol. The safest were found to be Preston, Norwich and Ipswich.

When it came to household accidents, the riskiest cities were Hove, Milton Keynes and Brighton. The safest were Manchester, Leeds and Liverpool.

15.

Qualification and Associations

Landlord Qualifications

There is currently no general requirement for landlords to have any particular qualifications, to register with local authorities (except where licensing applies), or to belong to any professional bodies or associations. Apart from dealing with deposits as laid down by law, landlords do not have to operate particular accounts or even take out particular insurance.

However, there are a number of landlord associations to which they can belong, and accreditation schemes with which they can choose to register. This is usually worthwhile and membership can be offset against tax.

Landlord Associations

Whether or not they choose to seek accreditation, it is a good idea for landlords to seek out and build on the experiences of other landlords. This is most easily done via a landlord association.

In general the advantages of joining an association include access to meetings where ideas and information can be shared with other landlords, access to updates, courses and services, and having an advocate for landlord interests.

The leading national landlord associations are currently:

- The Residential Landlords Association, a Manchester-based group with a membership of 8,800 and national coverage – **www.rla.org.uk**.

- The National Landlords Association, a London-based group which represents over 19,000 fee-paying individual and corporate members throughout the UK – **www.landlords.org.uk**.

Both the RLA and NLA have local associations attached to them. There are also a number of independent local landlord associations (London and the South East are covered by branches of the national association), including:

Devon – **www.devonlandlords.co.uk**

East Midlands – **www.empo.co.uk**

Eastern – **www.easternlandlords.org.uk**

Humber – **www.hdla.net**

North Staffordshire – **nsla.co.uk**

North West – **www.nwla.co.uk**

North West Property Owners – **www.nwpoa.co.uk**

Sheffield & District – **www.sadla.org.uk**

Southwest – **www.landlordssouthwest.co.uk**

West Country – **www.wlainfo.co.uk**

Yorkshire Coast – **www.ycrla.com**

Scotland has the Scottish Association of Landlords, based in Edinburgh and with 12 local branches – **www.scottishlandlords.com**

Northern Ireland has the Landlords' Association of Northern Ireland – **www.lani.org.uk**

Landlord Accreditation Schemes

Both the NLA and RLA have their own accreditation schemes for landlords, as do (growing) numbers of local authorities and universities.

For the authorities these provide the advantage of knowing that the accommodation offered by members is up to the standard required and of giving them a means of helping to improve those standards. For landlords the advantage of membership lies in both the help and advice that becomes available and in the kudos of belonging to an accreditation scheme – which can only assist with marketing. When it comes to universities, those that have accreditation schemes are also likely to assist landlords in finding student tenants.

Incentives offered vary from scheme to scheme but may include access to a liaison officer who can help landlords deal with local authority departments, consultation on proposals that may affect landlords, access to renovation grants and loans, and reduced landlord licence fees.

Membership of accreditation schemes is voluntary. Belonging to a scheme means agreeing to abide by laid-down standards and codes dealing with the management and/or condition of rental property.

There is a government booklet on 'Landlord accreditation' available to download from **www.communities.gov.uk**.

ANUK – the Accreditation Network UK (**www.anuk.org.uk**) has a directory of accreditation schemes listed by area.

The National Landlords Association moved forward with its own accreditation scheme in 2010, announcing that 173 UK local authorities had "expressed a strong interest" in becoming involved. This was after completion of a six-month pilot conducted with five local authorities.

"NLA Accreditation works with local councils to provide up-to-date information and support to landlords in their area," it explained. "It is an ideal way for responsible landlords to be able to promote their services as a 'good landlord' to tenants, who can easily verify a landlord's commitment to ongoing professional development and the highest standards in their letting business.

"NLA Accreditation offers a structured approach to landlord development by utilising online and face-to-face courses. It is free for local authorities to participate in NLA Accreditation and also helps to increase the supply of good accommodation. This is important as more and more councils are looking to private landlords to provide much-needed housing."

More information about NLA Accreditation can be found on the website **www.goodlandlord.org.uk**.

Scotland has a government-backed national Landlord Accreditation Scheme, which was established in 2008 after successful pilots in local authorities.

There are also local schemes in Fife (Charter for Private Landlords), Dumfries and Galloway (Quality Rent South West), Dundee, Edinburgh (**www.edinburghlandlordaccreditation.co.uk**) and South Ayrshire (under review).

16.

Scotland and Northern Ireland

Scotland has its own laws, rules and regulations. Although similar to those that apply in England and Wales, they are not identical and, when it comes to landlord and tenant law, sometimes anticipate what is later to become English law.

The content of this guide applies to England and Wales and only to Scotland and Northern Ireland where specifically stated as such.

However, the Scottish Executive has published guidance for Scottish landlords and also a portfolio of forms, all of which can be accessed at **www.scotland.gov.uk**.

Likewise not all laws coincide in England and Northern Ireland. For Northern Ireland's Department for Social Development booklets for landlords, visit **www.dsdni.gov.uk**. The website of the Rent Officer for Northern Ireland can be found at **www.rentofficer-ni.gov.uk**.

Scotland

A major difference for landlords in Scotland is that deposits do not at present have to be protected in a government-approved scheme, although the Scottish Executive has this under review (its Safeguarding Tenancy Deposits working group has issued a number of discussion papers). Another important difference is that all landlords are required to register with their local authority (details on **www.landlordregistrationscotland.gov.uk**).

Also, since 2009 landlords have had a duty, under the Homelessness (etc) Scotland Act 2003, to inform their local authority when commencing possession proceedings against tenants.

Different rules apply to the condition of privately rented houses.

In general Scottish landlords have a duty to ensure their properties meet the *repairing standard*. To do this:

- they must be wind and watertight and in all other respects reasonably fit for human habitation

- the structure and exterior of the house (including drains, gutters and external pipes) must be in a reasonable state of repair and in proper working order

- installations in the house for the supply of water, gas and electricity and for sanitation, space heating and heating water must be in a reasonable state of repair and in proper working order

- any fixtures, fittings and appliances provided by the landlord under the tenancy must be in a reasonable state of repair and in proper working order

- any furnishings provided by the landlord under the tenancy must be capable of being used safely for the purpose for which they are designed

- they must have satisfactory provision for detecting fires and for giving warning in the event of fire or suspected fire.

If a rented house does not meet that standard, and the landlord refuses to carry out the necessary repairs, tenants can apply to the Private Rented Housing Panel (which took over from the Rent Assessment Panel) for Scotland for a decision on whether the landlord has failed to comply with his or her duty. Landlords can, if necessary, be ordered to carry out the necessary repairs with various penalties applying if they do not.

More details on this are available from the panel's website at **www.prhpscotland.gov.uk**.

The repairing standard, landlord registration and HMO licensing are covered in the booklet: 'Assured Tenancies in Scotland – Your Rights and Responsibilities, A Guide for Private Landlords and

Tenants' (available from the Scottish government website: **www.scotland.gov.uk**).

Before it was abolished in 2008 (most of its functions were transferred to the Scottish government's Housing and Regeneration directorate and to the new Scottish Housing Regulator), Communities Scotland published *The Scottish National Core Standards and Good Practice Guidance for Private Landlords*. This provide "a framework for setting and monitoring the achievement of good management practice by private landlords" and was based on "current legislation, good practice and common sense".

According to the standards document it could be used by private landlords to "benchmark themselves" and also in the development of local voluntary accreditation schemes based on partnership between local authorities, landlord organisations and other stakeholders.

Included in the document was a model tenancy agreement compliant with Scottish law, together with information about Scottish landlord responsibilities and best practice. These included:

Communication with the tenant: Landlords should communicate clearly, promptly and informatively with tenants on any matter that affects the property, its management and the tenants' safe and peaceful occupation. All information provided by landlords should be written in plain English and, when requested, landlords should provide summary translations of written information in relevant minority languages, Braille or large print.

Complaints: At the outset of a tenancy landlords should advise tenants in writing of the way or ways that any complaints should be registered. Records should be kept by landlords of complaints made by the tenants or third parties together with the outcome of the complaint.

Equality issues, complaints and disputes: Landlords must ensure no person or group of people is treated less favourably than any other because of his, her or their race, colour, ethnic or national origin, sex, disability or sexual orientation. Neither may landlords unreasonably withhold consent to tenants to adapt rented accommodation to meet the needs of disabled occupants.

Fit and Proper to let: Landlords are required to be registered with the local authority's Private Landlord Registration Scheme.

Tenancy agreement: Where the let is on an assured or short-assured tenancy, the tenant must be given a written tenancy agreement setting out the terms of the let and any relevant notices, and setting out the name and current address of the landlord and/or agent. This agreement should set out the rights and responsibilities of both landlord and tenant in clear and lawful terms and must be properly executed by the signatures of the landlord (or agent) and tenant, and one witness, who must include his or her address.

Rent and other charges: Where rent is paid weekly, a rent book must be issued and receipted for each weekly payment made.

Possession: Landlords must use the correct legal procedures when seeking possession.

Anti-social behaviour: Landlords must take lawful forms of action to resolve any issues regarding the anti-social behaviour by occupants and visitors to their rental properties.

Deposits and initial payments: Where deposits are required, they must be no more than the equivalent of two months' rent and the tenant should receive a written statement of what the deposit (or guarantee) covers and a statement of what will be required, or have to be in place, for the full deposit to be returned at the end of the tenancy. The first rent payment and any deposit should only be taken at the point the tenancy agreement is signed. A reasonable exception is where both parties agree that a holding deposit is taken and for which a receipt is issued. Any administration charges to a new tenant must reflect only actual costs incurred. No charge must be made for drawing up or copying the tenancy agreement.

Minimum property standard: Tenants' accommodation must meet required standards. Landlords should take all reasonable steps to ensure proper maintenance of the common elements of the building, which are a shared responsibility with other co-owners, and have a duty to repair and maintain their rental properties at the start of the tenancy and at all times during the tenancy. When notified or on becoming aware of defects, landlords must put matters right within a reasonable time. Landlords must inspect their properties before each tenancy starts so as to identify any work necessary to comply with the Repairing Standard and also provide tenants with written information about the effect of the Repairing Standard in relation to the tenancy. Tenants should be provided with information on how to approach the Private Rented Housing Panel and in what circumstances.

Gas safety: Landlords must comply with current Gas Safety (Installation and Use) Regulations by arranging annual gas safety checks to be completed by a Gas Safe registered contractor, and gas safety certificates obtained (and copies provided to tenants). Landlords should ensure all servicing, repairs and replacements are completed by a Gas Safe registered contractor. Records of safety checks must be retained for two years at least.

Electricity: Landlords should take all reasonable steps to ensure that all electrical appliances supplied as part of the let are safe to use.

Furnishings and furniture safety: All furnishings and furniture supplied as part of a let must comply with relevant parts of the Furniture and Furnishings (Fire) (Safety) Regulations.

Energy Performance Certificates: An Energy Performance Certificate must be provided when a property is let for the first time or when a new tenant moves in.

Houses in Multiple Occupation: All HMO properties must hold a current HMO licence.

More detailed information and advice about renting in Scotland can be found on the Better Renting website: **www.betterrentingscotland.com**

Northern Ireland

Effective from April 2007, The Private Tenancies (Northern Ireland) Order 2006 introduced a new structure for the private rented sector in Northern Ireland.

- New tenancies were defined according to their fitness for habitation – an unfit tenancy was made subject to rent control until made fit.

- District councils were made responsible for inspecting tenancies for fitness and given powers to ensure that unfitness and serious disrepair is addressed.

- Controlled rents are now based on a number of factors including the condition of the property, the equivalent Housing Executive rent for a similar dwelling and the general level of rents in the area.

- Restricted and regulated tenancies retained their protection. Existing tenants were confirmed as having a tenancy for life but with only one further succession possible (rather than two as before).

There are to be no more protected tenancies. On vacancy, all protected tenancies become decontrolled so that if fit for habitation the rent is not subject to control when the property is re-let.

As well as having rent books, new tenants have to be supplied with a written statement of the terms of their tenancy. Where a tenancy agreement fails to clarify repairing obligations, the law provides default terms.

The provisions of the Rent Order, which allowed for annual rent increases for registered rents, was repealed on 1 April 2007. To increase controlled rents after this date, landlords have had to apply to the Rent Officer for Northern Ireland (**www.rentofficer-ni.gov.uk**).

Whether or not a rental property is deemed fit for habitation depends on whether or not it meets the statutory fitness standard set out in the Housing (Northern Ireland) Order 1981 (as amended by the Housing (NI) Order 1992). To meet the standard a dwelling must:

- be structurally stable

- be free from serious disrepair

- be free from dampness prejudicial to the health of the occupants

- have adequate provision for lighting, heating and ventilation

- have an adequate piped supply of wholesome water

- have satisfactory facilities in the house for the preparation and cooking of food, including a sink with a satisfactory supply of hot and cold water

- have a suitably located water closet for the exclusive use of the occupants

- have a suitably located fixed bath or shower and wash hand basin, for the exclusive use of the occupants, each of which is provided with a satisfactory supply of hot and cold water

- have an effective system for the draining of foul waste and surface water.

There are a number of free booklets for landlords that can be downloaded from Northern Ireland's Department for Social Development website (**www.dsdni.gov.uk**). They include: 'Protection Against Harassment and Illegal Eviction – A Guide for Private Landlords and Tenants in Northern Ireland'', 'Protected and Statutory Tenancies – A Guide for Private Landlords', 'Tenants in Northern Ireland', 'Repairs – A Guide for Private Landlords and Tenants in Northern Ireland' and 'Private Tenancies – A Guide for Private Landlords and Tenants in Northern Ireland'.

Meanwhile NI direct (**www.nidirect.gov.uk**) has a list of landlord obligations. These set out responsibilities for:

- Compliance with the Disability Discrimination Order (NI) 2006, the Sex Discrimination (Northern Ireland) Order 1976 and the Race Relations (NI) Order 1997

- repairs to the structure and exterior of rental properties, their heating and hot water systems, basins, sinks, baths and other sanitary ware

- the safety of gas and electrical appliances

- the fire safety of furniture and furnishings provided as part of the tenancy

- ensuring that rental properties are fit for habitation

- repairing and keeping in working order the room and water heating equipment

- maintaining the common areas in multi-occupancy dwellings.

For additional information on landlord responsibilities, landlords are advised to check the Housing Executive's website (**www.nihe.gov.uk**).

Unlike landlords in England and Scotland, those in Northern Ireland must always provide a rent book. They may also be responsible for paying local rates. This is the case where the capital value of the property is less than £55,000, or where it is between £55,001 and £150,000 and the rental frequency is less than quarterly. However, rate rebates are available.

17.

Ten Golden Rules

Letting is a business and should be approached in a businesslike way. Here are ten rules that will help:

1. Know your market

Find out what type of property is in demand and what is not, what type of property is likely to attract which type of tenant and what rents are likely to be achievable. It may pay in the longer term not to ask for the absolute highest possible rent and thereby have a wider choice of possible tenants.

2. Choose property carefully

Type of property and location are extremely important. They will dictate whether you are able to let at a viable rent, to whom, and whether you are likely to see long-term capital gains. Use your market knowledge to choose properties at least as carefully as you would choose your own home.

3. Choose tenants carefully

Tenants will be entrusted with your (substantial) investment. Do not let them move in without knowing who they are (by conducting identity checks) and that they are likely to stick to their side of the renting bargain (conduct credit checks, take references and ask probing questions).

4. Do not overstretch your finances

Borrowing heavily could pay off when property prices are on the rise, but could be disastrous when they are not. Letting is long term; so make sure you are prepared for this and remember that property cannot easily be sold at the drop of a hat – especially when times are tight.

5. Know and follow the rules and regulations

Make sure you know your responsibilities as a landlord and fulfil them. Among other things this means obtaining licences where required, keeping property up to required standards, protecting tenancy deposits, conducting annual gas safety checks, not being discriminatory in dealings with tenants, dealing with personal information according to data-protection legislation and having energy performance certificates.

6. Join a landlord association

Benefit from the experience of other landlords. Members of landlords' associations will have collectively experienced virtually all of the problems that landlords can face, and they will be willing to pass on the lessons learned. Belonging to a landlords' association will also give you access to training courses and help keep you up to date.

7. Protect your identity

Make sure none of your own personal data can be accessed by tenants – this means making sure no personal information is left in rental properties (other than your contact details), not allowing personal mail to be sent to a rental property (even if this was your previous residence) and not allowing utilities to be supplied to rental properties in your own name.

8. Keep proper records

Make sure your records are adequate for tax purposes but also sufficiently comprehensive to deal with disputes with suppliers and tenants (especially concerning tenancy deposits and unpaid rent). Besides keeping accounts and copies of tenancy agreements, this means filing away such things as tenant application forms, details of tenants' employers and next of kin, detailed inventories, preferably backed with photographic evidence, and receipts for keys and the like.

9. Insure your risks

Assess the risks you face and decide which, if the worst comes to the worst, you can afford to deal with from your own resources. Some will be too large and these you should insure – including property, third party liability, and perhaps loss of rent.

10. Keep up to date

Make sure you keep up to date both with the rental market and with the latest changes in laws and regulations affecting your responsibilities. The best way to do this is via membership of a landlords' association, making contact with your local authority, reading landlord magazines and visiting trusted websites and forums. After all, the cost of keeping up to date is allowable for tax purposes as a deduction from taxable income.

Jargon Buster

Accelerated possession procedure (APP)

A cheap and straightforward way for landlords to gain possession of their property without a court hearing. Unless it considers a hearing is necessary, the court will make its decision based solely on documents provided by the landlord and tenant. This procedure can only be used where there is a written tenancy agreement and the tenant has been given notice. The procedure cannot be used to claim for arrears of rent.

Accreditation

See 'Landlord accreditation'

Annual percentage rate (APR)

A standard measure of the cost of borrowing, including interest charges and other fees, which must be shown on all UK loan advertisements.

Arrangement fee

Fee charged by some lenders and intermediaries for access to particular mortgage deals, often fixed-rate or discounted-rate mortgages. May be payable in advance or added to loan.

Association of Residential Letting Agents (ARLA)

Professional association for letting agents, which operates a code of practice and bond scheme that protects the clients (landlords) of ARLA members.

Assured shorthold tenancy (AST)

A form of tenancy that assures the landlord's right to repossess the property at the end of the term specified in the tenancy agreement, which can be for any length of time (although whatever the agreement says, tenants who do not breach its terms can stay in the property for at least the first six months). To gain possession the landlord must serve a notice under section 21 of the Housing Act 1988, giving a minimum of two months' notice. Landlords may also apply for possession during the course of a tenancy on various grounds for possession. Some give the court no option but to grant possession. Excepting rentals with very low or very high rents (the figure is £100,000 a year as from 1 October 2010), ASTs are the default type of tenancy for all new tenancies unless otherwise specified.

Assured tenancy

A form of tenancy introduced under the 1988 Housing Act for property let out as a separate dwelling and used as the tenant's only or main home. An assured tenancy will generally allow the tenant to stay in occupation until either he or she decides to leave or the landlord obtains a possession order.

Bank base rate

Also known as *repro rate*, *base rate* and *bank rate*, this is the rate set each month by the Bank of England's Monetary Policy Committee as the rate at which it will lend to retail banks. It is used as the benchmark for many other interest rates, including personal loans and mortgages.

Buy-to-let mortgage

A type of mortgage designed to allow the recipient to purchase residential property for letting.

Capped rate mortgages

Mortgage loans in which the rate of interest is variable but guaranteed not to exceed a specified level for a set period.

Commonhold

Form of tenure created by the Commonhold and Leasehold Reform Act 2002, in which leaseholders in a property jointly hold the freehold through an association.

Conveyancing

Legal process of transferring the ownership of property, typically when it is bought and sold.

County Court Judgement (CCJ)

A judgement for unpaid debt recorded at a County Court and which will show up when a credit check is undertaken.

Court Service

This is a publicly available service that provides online access to various forms that landlords may require when commencing proceedings for possession. The Court Service website also has guidance on such subjects as dealing with squatters. Forms available to download include N5 for use in possession claims, and N5B for use in the accelerated possession procedure.

Credit reference agency

Companies that can provide credit information about individuals (including CCJs) and confirmation of addresses included on the electoral register.

Deposit protection scheme

See 'Tenancy deposit protection'.

Discounted-rate mortgage

A mortgage in which the lender agrees a fixed discount off the normal variable rate for a guaranteed period of time. Likely to include penalties for early redemption.

Discretionary grounds for possession

Grounds that may be cited in possession proceedings which allow the court discretion as to whether or not to grant possession – there are also eight mandatory grounds for possession.

The discretionary grounds cover circumstances in which: the landlord has offered suitable alternative accommodation on the same basis; there are rent arrears but not of more than eight weeks (or two months if the rent is paid monthly, or one quarter if paid quarterly); there are persistent and continuing rent arrears; the tenant has breached the terms of the tenancy agreement; the tenant has neglected or damaged the property or has sub-let; the tenant is causing nuisance to neighbours; furniture supplied under the tenancy agreement has been damaged; the accommodation is linked to employment which has ended; and the tenant has knowingly or recklessly made false statements on which the landlord has relied in granting a tenancy.

Easement

A right, such as a right of way, which the owner of one property has over an adjoining property.

Empty dwelling management order (EDMO)

An EDMO is an order that, once approved by an independent property tribunal, gives a local authority power to take possession of an empty property so as to bring it back into use. Ownership does not change, but the council can do most things the owner would normally be entitled to do.

There are two types of EDMO. An interim EDMO lasts for no more than 12 months, during which time the council must try to work with the owner to agree a way of getting your property back into use. It must ask the owner's permission before it can let the property. If that permission is not given, the council may make a final EDMO, which can last for up to seven years. If it does not issue a final EDMO, it must end the interim EDMO and hand back possession of the property to the owner.

Energy performance certificate (EPC)

An assessment of household energy usage and the extent to which this can be lowered. Certificates give properties a rating from A to G, presented graphically in much the same style as used for fridges, washing machines and other white goods. Residential rental properties must have a certificate that is not more than ten years old.

Eviction

In most cases it is illegal for a landlord to evict a tenant without a court order. The Protection from Eviction Act 1977 also protects tenants against being forced to leave a property through harassment, such as threats or physical violence, or through withdrawal of services such as disconnecting the electrical supply or refusing to carry out vital repairs. Also see 'Grounds for possession'.

Fair rent

Rent determined by the Rent Service, applicable to regulated tenancies and set according to local market conditions – but with any increase on a previously registered fair rent capped (except where the landlord has made substantial improvements to the property) by a formula based on the rate of inflation.

Final management order (FMO)

Orders which local authorities can obtain to extend the powers to take over management of rental properties that have been subject to an IMO (see below) for a further five years.

Financial Services Authority (FSA)

The Financial Services Authority has statutory responsibility for regulating the financial services sector, including the sale of private homebuyer mortgages, but not businesses or buy-to-let mortgages.

Fixed-interest rate mortgage

A mortgage loan in which the interest rate is fixed for a set period of time whether or not the base rate goes up or down. There are likely to be penalties included for early redemption.

Fixtures

Articles such as radiators, boilers and baths, attached to the house itself and deemed to be part of it.

Flexible mortgages

Mortgages allowing for the possibility of part redemptions and repayment holidays without penalty.

Freehold

Indefinite ownership of a property as opposed to a leasehold tenure which is for a fixed period. The relatively recently introduced commonhold tenure combines elements of freehold and leasehold.

Good repair

Landlords are required by law to keep their rented properties in good repair and fit for human habitation. Should local environmental health officers rule that a tenant's health has been affected by the state of living conditions, he or she would be able to claim compensation from their landlord. Also see HHSRS below.

Grounds for possession

There are 17 grounds for possession laid down in the Housing Act 1988, as amended by the Housing Act 1996, that may be cited in possession proceedings against a tenant. Eight are mandatory grounds which oblige the court to award possession provided the landlord has complied with the procedure set out in the Housing Acts and has served the tenant with the appropriate notices. Nine are discretionary, allowing the court some leeway. Landlords may also seek possession when it can be demonstrated that a tenant is no longer using the accommodation as his or her principal home.

Harassment

Harassment is a criminal offence under the Protection from Eviction Act 1977. The term refers to acts by a landlord or agent likely to interfere with the peace or comfort of a tenant or involve the withdrawal or withholding of services reasonably required for occupation. Harassment can include the landlord continually visiting the property or contacting tenants.

Health and safety rating system (HHSRS)

A risk-based method of assessment which councils are required to use when evaluating a property's safety. This may be undertaken following a complaint, or for other reasons, such as when a HMO licence is applied for. The HHSRS is primarily concerned with those matters which can properly be considered the responsibility of the owner (or landlord). There are 29 headings under which risk is assessed. Should hazards be identified under any of these, councils must go on to assess the likelihood of those hazards crystallising and causing harm, and the probable severity of any such harm. The assessment culminates in a *hazard rating* for the property. There are four classes of harm, of which *category one* is the most severe. These are risks that could lead to death, permanent paralysis below the neck, regular severe pneumonia, or 80% burns or worse. Local authorities have a duty to take action on category-one hazards and the power to take action on category-two hazards. This applies to all properties, whether owner-occupied or rented, although landlords are the most likely to be affected.

Housing benefit

Housing benefit is a means-tested benefit available to help people who are on state benefits or who have low incomes pay their rent. The current form of housing benefit is known as local housing allowance.

Houses in multiple occupation (HMOs)

In England and Wales HMOs are defined under the Housing Act 2004 as:

- entire houses or flats let to three or more tenants from two or more households who share a kitchen, bathroom or toilet

- houses converted entirely into bedsits or other accommodation that is not self-contained, let to three or more tenants who form two or more households and who share kitchen, bathroom or toilet facilities

- converted houses containing one or more flats which are not wholly self-contained, occupied by three or more tenants who form two or more households and who share facilities

- buildings which have been converted entirely into self-contained flats, but where the conversion did not meet the standards of the 1991 Building Regulations and more than one third of the flats are let on short-term tenancies.

In each case the property must be used as the tenants' only or main residence and it should be used solely or mainly to house tenants. Properties let to students and migrant workers will be treated as such tenants' only or main residence, and the same will apply to properties which are used as domestic refuges. All of these properties could be subject to mandatory or additional licensing requirements, but not all are. It is only those that are of three or more storeys with five or more occupants that in fact require a licence.

In Scotland HMOs are defined as houses used as the only or principal residence of three or more qualifying persons from three or more families. A *house* includes any building, or any part of a building, occupied as a separate dwelling. The legislation covers not only ordinary shared houses or flats and bedsits, but all residential accommodation, including hostels, student halls of residence, and staff accommodation in hotels or hospitals.

Separate units within a building which share use of a toilet, personal washing facilities or cooking facilities are taken to form part of a single house.

Two people are members of the same family if they are partners (including same sex couples) or related, including relationships by marriage or by half blood, and children who are fostered, adopted or otherwise brought up as a member of the family.

Houses in multiple occupation – mandatory licensing

In England and Wales it is an offence, punishable by fines of up to £20,000, to let without a licence properties that are caught by the mandatory licensing provisions of the Housing Act 2004. Those rental properties that require a licence under the Act are HMOs of three or more storeys, with five or more occupants who form two or more households – households being partners and relatives living together – using shared facilities such as kitchens and bathrooms.

Properties do not have to be entire houses but can be part of buildings let to five or more unrelated people even if the tenants have signed a joint tenancy agreement. Attics and basements are included in the storey count if they are used as living accommodation.

In Scotland it is a criminal offence to give permission for a house to be occupied as an HMO without a licence. The maximum penalty is currently £5,000. The application for a licence must be made by the owner, even if the property is leased to or managed by another person or organisation

Housing Ombudsman Service (HOS)

The Housing Ombudsman Service is set up by law to look at complaints about providers of housing registered with the service. These include all housing associations and some private landlords and management agents. The service is free, independent and impartial. There is a searchable membership database on the HOS website at **www.housing-ombudsman.org.uk**.

HMRC

Her Majesty's Revenue & Customs, the UK tax authority for personal and corporate taxes and for VAT.

Improvement notice

A notice requiring a landlord or property owner to undertake work where an environmental health officer has found that the property fails to meet the requirements of the Health and Safety Rating System (HHSRS) – see above.

Interest-only mortgage

Mortgage loan on which no capital repayments are made for a specified time or until redemption.

Interim management order (IMO)

Orders which local authorities can obtain to take over management of rental properties that are licensed, or ought to be licensed, where licensing requirements and conditions are not being met. IMOs are for 12 months and allow the authority to do anything in relation to the house which could have been done by the landlord.

Landlord accreditation

A growing number of local authorities are introducing voluntary private landlord accreditation schemes, as are universities for student lets, and landlord associations. Generally landlords who sign up agree to adhere to given standards in return for being able to say they are accredited.

Accreditation Network UK (ANUK) is a network of professionals and associations that promote accreditation.

Landlord's energy saving allowance

Tax allowance available to landlords that covers the cost of loft insulation, cavity wall insulation, solid wall insulation, draught proofing, hot water system insulation, and floor insulation.

Landlord licensing

In England and Wales, landlords must obtain licences from local authorities for HMO properties of three or more storeys with five or more occupants who form two or more households – households being partners and relatives living together – using shared facilities such as kitchens and bathrooms. The licensing process includes assessment of whether or not they are *fit and proper* to be HMO landlords and apply adequate management standards.

In Scotland all landlords must register with their local authorities under the Antisocial Behaviour etc. (Scotland) Act 2004. Letting property without registering could result in a fine of up to £5,000 and to rental income being withheld.

Land Registry

Official registry of property titles containing the world's largest property database, guaranteeing ownership of £1,300bn worth of property. The Land Registration Act 2002, which came into effect in October 2003, gives owners of registered property greater protection against squatters and allows them to block applications for adverse possession, with time allowed for recovery of possession.

Leasehold

Ownership of property for a fixed term granted by lease. The lease sets out details of rents and obligations such as repairs. Other possible tenures include freehold and commonhold.

Leasehold valuation tribunals (LVTs)

Rent assessment panels, which determine specified aspects of leasehold disputes under the Landlord and Tenant Acts of 1985 and 1987, as amended by the Housing Act 1996.

LIBOR

LIBOR is the interest rate applicable to some loans and mortgages. It is the London Inter Bank Offered Rate at which banks lend money to each other. LIBOR changes daily and a LIBOR-linked mortgage will normally be adjusted every three months.

Loan to value (LTV)

Size of mortgage as a percentage of the value of a property. Many lenders offer more favourable deals to customers who are seeking lower LTVs.

Local government ombudsmen

The local government ombudsmen investigate complaints of injustice arising from maladministration by local authorities and certain other bodies. There are three local government ombudsmen in England and they each deal with complaints from different parts of the country. They investigate complaints about most council matters including housing.

Local housing allowance (LHA)

The current form of housing benefit, based on rents payable within local broad rental market areas (in which claimants could reasonably be expected to live) and the housing needs of recipients. The benefit is generally paid direct to recipients. Changes announced to take effect in April 2011 were designed to cut the anticipated cost of LHA by nearly 9%.

Mandatory grounds for possession

Grounds that may be cited in possession proceedings linked to an assured tenancy which, provided the correct procedures have been followed and notices given, require the court to grant possession. In brief, the mandatory grounds cover situations where: the landlord requires the property for personal occupation; a mortgage lender is foreclosing the mortgage; property let for a fixed period is required for return to holiday letting; an educational institution requires return of a student let; a religious body requires return of its property for an alternative tenant; the landlord wishes to demolish, reconstruct or redevelop the property; a landlord wishes to claim possession against the resident heir of a tenant who has died; and the rent is in arrears by eight weeks or more (two months if it is paid monthly, or one quarter if paid quarterly).

Mortgage

A deed pledging freehold or leasehold property as security for a loan (also legally called a charge). If payments are not made according to the terms of the mortgage and fall into arrears, the mortgage issuer will be able to foreclose, claim the property and sell it on to recover the outstanding amount. The term *mortgage* is also often used to mean the loan that is secured by a mortgage.

National Approved Letting Scheme (NALS)

The National Approved Letting Scheme is a government-backed accreditation scheme which all letting agents and letting management agents can join. In doing so they agree to meet defined standards of customer service, to maintain necessary insurances to protect clients' money, and to have customer complaints procedures in place offering independent redress.

The scheme is supported by the Association of Residential Letting Agents, National Association of Estate Agents and Royal Institution of Chartered Surveyors.

National Association of Estate Agents (NAEA)

The largest professional estate agency organisation in the UK. Representing nearly 10,000 members, the NAEA is committed to raising professional standards across all aspects of the property market for the benefit of member agents and ultimately the home-moving public.

National Inspection Council for Electrical Installation Contracting (NICEIC)

An independent consumer safety organisation that has also been the electrical contracting industry's voluntary regulatory body for electrical safety matters for more than 45 years.

Building regulations require that most substantial electrical work is carried out by a *competent person* such as a contractor approved by the NICEIC.

National Landlords Association (NLA)

The National Landlords Association is the largest UK association of private landlords, protecting and promoting their interests and providing membership benefits such as fact sheets, newsletters, insurance discounts, meetings and workshops, and favourable terms with selected suppliers of advice and services.

Noise abatement notice

The notice requiring noisy activity to stop or requiring steps to be taken to reduce the noise (such as insulation or volume control) issued when an environmental health officer finds the level of noise from a property to be prejudicial to health or a nuisance.

Non-resident landlords scheme

A scheme for taxing the UK rental income of non-resident landlords. The scheme requires UK letting agents to deduct basic rate tax from any rent they collect for non-resident landlords. If non-resident landlords don't have UK letting agents acting for them, and the rent is more than £100 a week, their tenants must deduct the tax. When working out the amount of tax, the letting agent/tenant can take off deductible expenses.

Letting agents and/or tenants don't have to deduct tax if HMRC tells them not to. HMRC will tell an agent/tenant not to deduct tax if non-resident landlords have successfully applied to it for approval to receive rents with no tax deduction. But even though the rent may be paid with no tax deducted, it remains liable to UK tax. So non-resident landlords must include it in their tax returns.

Notice to quit

A notice to quit, or more properly a *notice requiring repossession*, issued under section 21 of the Housing Act 1988 is notice to a tenant that he or she must vacate a property at the end of an assured shorthold tenancy agreement. There is no prescribed form for the notice but it must specify the date after which the tenant is to give up possession. At least two months' notice is required and possession may not be required until expiry of the first six months of the tenancy.

Ombudsman for estate agents (OEA)

The property ombudsman is charged with resolving disputes between property sales and letting agents who have joined the OEA scheme and their clients, including landlords. The service is free and independent.

Since October 2008, all estate agents have been required to register with an estate agents redress scheme, such as the OEA, that has been approved by the Office of Fair Trading (OFT) and which investigates complaints against estate agents. Lettings and property management agents are not required to register in this way but may do so.

Periodic tenancy

A periodic tenancy comes into being when a landlord does nothing to reclaim possession at the end of an original assured shorthold tenancy and allows the tenants to remain without issuing a new tenancy agreement. The terms and conditions of the original assured shorthold tenancy agreement remain in place, as does the right of the landlord to bring the tenancy to an end by service of the required two months' notice.

Possession

See 'Mandatory grounds for possession, 'Assured shorthold tenancy', 'Discretionary grounds for possession', 'Grounds for possession' and 'Section 21'.

Quiet enjoyment

Allowing tenants quiet enjoyment of their rented homes is an implied term within *any* letting agreement and affords tenants the right to uninterrupted use of the property during the course of their tenancy without interference from the landlord or the landlord's agents.

Registered rent

Rent included on the publicly available Rent Register as determined by a rent officer or rent assessment panel recording the maximum that can be charged until a new determination is agreed or the tenant leaves.

Regulated tenancy

Most continuing private tenancies entered into before 15 January 1989 are regulated tenancies under the Rent Act 1977. This means that the tenant has long-term security of tenure and that both the landlord and the tenant have the right to have a fair rent registered for the tenancy by an independent rent officer. Both also have a right to appeal to a rent assessment committee if they are dissatisfied with the rent officer's decision.

Once a rent is registered, the landlord cannot normally charge a higher rent without reapplying to the rent officer and a new application for registration is not possible for two years unless there is a relevant change of circumstances. The Housing Act 1988, which introduced assured and assured shorthold tenancies at market rents for most new lettings on or after 15 January 1989, did not change existing tenants' rights to security of tenure and rent control.

Rent assessment committees (RACs)

When a landlord or tenant of a regulated tenancy has objected to the rent assessed by a rent officer, the case will be passed to a residential property tribunal service and will be heard by one of its rent assessment committees – it also refers to them as panels – to decide the fair rent. Tenants with assured tenancies may also apply to an RAC for a determination of the open market rent they should be paying. They may also apply if the landlord serves notice of a proposed rent increase.

Rent Service

Formerly an executive agency of the Department for Work and Pensions, the Rent Service was transferred to the Valuation Office Agency on 1 April 2009. VOA is now responsible for rental valuations for housing benefit purposes, making fair rent determinations, and advising local authorities about the effects on rent of housing renovation grant applications by landlords.

Rental yields

Precise definitions can vary but the gross rental yield is usually taken to be the annual rent of a property as a percentage of its capital value or acquisition price. The net rental yield is the annual rent after deducting expenses as a percentage of capital value or acquisition price. The rental return or capital return is the annual income from renting, less the costs, plus annual capital appreciation as a percentage of the original investment in the property.

Repayment mortgage

A mortgage loan in which the borrower pays a set amount each month comprising an element of both interest and capital repayment and calculated to fully pay off the mortgage loan by its expiry date.

Residential Landlords Association (RLA)

National association of private landlords with a membership of over 8,000 and head offices in Manchester. The RLA is active in lobbying government on behalf of private landlords and provides a range of service members. Its website is at **www.rla.org.uk**

Residential Property Tribunal Service (RPTS)

An independent body which aims to provide a fair and accessible tribunal service to help landlords, tenants and leaseholders settle disputes about rents and about leasehold property. RPTS, whose remit covers England, comprises five regional rent assessment panels, each covering a different geographical part of the country – London; Southern England; Northern England; the Midlands; and Eastern England.

Royal Institution of Chartered Surveyors (RICS)

The professional body for chartered surveyors, whose members work in all aspects of real estate – including letting, construction and associated environmental issues. RICS has 110,000 members globally and represents, regulates and promotes the work of property professionals throughout 120 countries.

Schedule A

Letting income is taxed under what is known as 'Schedule A' (general trading income is assessed under Schedule D, and income from employment under Schedule E). Each schedule has its own rules for the calculation of taxable income. HMRC has an explanatory leaflet, IR150, which can be downloaded.

Section 21 Notice

See 'Notice to quit'.

Stamp duty (more formally stamp duty land tax - SDLT)

A government tax on transfer of property. Duty is levied according to the price of property being transferred, and for residential properties is currently nil for properties sold for up to £250,000, 1% of the full price for properties priced between £125,000 and £250,000 (but nil for first time buyers until 24 March 2012), 3% for those priced between £250,001 and £500,000, and 4% for those priced above £500,000. Once a transaction falls into the 1%, 3%, or 4% band, that rate applies to the whole of the purchase price.

Stamp duty of 1% is also payable on new leases and rental agreements where the *net present value* (NPV) of total rent over the period of the lease or agreement, plus any premium, exceeds £125,000. NPV is the total that will be received, discounted for expected inflation, taking account of the timing of payments: HMRC has a calculator on its website. In practice SDLT is only likely to be payable on new leases and rental agreements where the rent is very high, or the lease or agreement very long (say 99 years), or both.

Standard variable rate (SVR)

Rate of interest normally charged on variable rate mortgage loans. The rate will go up and down from time to time during the course of the mortgage, according to general interest rate movements.

Tenancy deposit protection

Any landlord taking a monetary deposit must safeguard it by participating in a tenancy deposit scheme. There are two types of scheme available – a custodial scheme which holds the deposit, and insured schemes whereby the landlord retains the deposit but pays an insurance premium. Both approaches include dispute resolution arrangements. Until deposits have been safeguarded by a scheme, landlords are unable to regain possession of the property using usual *notice only grounds*.

Tracker mortgage

Variable rate mortgage loan in which the interest rate is linked to an external market rate, such as the Bank of England base rate, rather than a rate set by the lender.

Valuation Office Agency (VOA)

The Valuation Office Agency (VOA) is an executive agency of HM Revenue & Customs (HMRC), with 85 offices spread throughout England, Wales and Scotland, employing around 4,300 people. In 2009 it took over the functions of the Rent Service and is now responsible, for rental valuations for housing benefit purposes and for making fair rent determinations, among other things.

Void Periods

Time, usually measured in days, when properties offered for rent remain without tenants.

Index

References to terms explained in the Jargon Buster are in bold.
References to real-life examples are in bold-italics.
References to legislation are in italics.

C

D

E